MMM1

Modern Music Masters – Oasis

Tom Boniface-Webb

DEDICATION

This book is dedicated to Donna Boniface-Webb,
Isabelle Boniface-Webb and
Abigail Boniface-Webb

CONTENTS

ACKNOWLEDGMENTS

Thank you to all the following, without whom this book would not have been possible:

Editor: Jo Haywood
Cover Design: Barry Parkinson at www.beepea.co.uk
Social Media: Margot Mills
Advice, support and good vibes: Jenny Natasha
eBook publishing: Ian Skillicorn
The Society of Authors
Interviews: Mat Whitecross, John Robb, Grant Gee, Mark Gill
Special thanks to the UK Official Charts Company, the most invaluable resource for this book series

Books in the Modern Music Masters Series:

Oasis
Blur
Pulp
Manic Street Preachers
The Verve
Suede

MMM1 – Oasis Spotify Playlist

Available at: MMM1 – Oasis

FOREWORD:

Like any good idea – the wheel, the car, TV, the internet, the mobile phone – the music of Oasis feels like it has always been part of our lives. By 1994, when their fledgling career was just beginning to take off, we already wondered how we managed this far without them and their music. The songs, the guitars and Liam's voice were familiar yet original, cementing themselves into the cultural fabric of British history, as important to the fans as the signing of the Magna Carta or the reformation. Just like The Beatles, The Rolling Stones, Blur, Radiohead, the Spice Girls, and Robbie Williams, the music of Oasis provides the ambient soundtrack to our lives, so deeply ingrained we often take its presence for granted.

This book is the first in a series, focusing on key musical artists. At just over 50,000 words, it's not an exhaustive history of Oasis. More in-depth books on the band include Paolo Hewitt's *Getting High: The Adventures of Oasis* (Dean Street Press, 1997), *Brothers* by biggest brother Paul Gallagher (Virgin Books, 1997), Ian Robertson's *Oasis: What's the Story?* (Penguin, 1996), *Some Might Say – The Definitive Story of Oasis* (This Day in Music Books, 2020) by Richard Bowes or, for a thorough in-depth look at *Definitely Maybe*, Alex Niven's *33⅓* (Bloomsbury, 2014). Rather, this book is an introduction to the band, shining a light on what still captivates so many around the world today.

There is a particular focus on the UK singles and albums charts, partly because studying them is a key indicator of popularity, but also because Oasis had a definitive effect on the charts. With eight number 1 singles and eight number 1 albums, they became one of Britain's most successful groups of all time, right up there with their heroes The Beatles.

With physical sales of music now at an all-time low, chart position is perhaps more important than ever in helping us gauge what is (and isn't) popular. With the singles chart now encompassing physical sales, downloads, streams and airplay, it captures exactly what people are listening to like never before.

Chart success, however, is not the only way to gauge an artist's impact and, as such, the story of each act runs on its own distinct set of rails. One band reaching number 56 in the singles chart can be every bit as important as another reaching number 3. Particularly if they manage it with no support from a record company or traditional promotion. Therefore, although this series of books focuses on the UK charts, each act will also be judged on their own merit. The intention is for the series to be immediately identifiable, a trusted friend to guide you along the distinct route plotted by each artist.

I hope you enjoy the journey with me.

A FEW WORDS FROM THE AUTHOR

Oasis were the first band that I truly loved. And the first band that I felt belonged to me. Growing up in Reading, I perhaps fitted the Blur mould better: semi-studious, art-schooly, southern and, most importantly, middle-class. But, while Blur did become one of my favourite bands, Oasis got to me first – and got me the deepest. It was around the time of the release of Wonderwall in October 1995. This song was everywhere: played on the radio every other song, in the local HMV record store my friends and I wandered around after school, in the cafe I worked in on Sunday mornings, on *Top of the Pops* every Thursday (and then Friday) evening. Soon afterwards, I bought *(What's the Story) Morning Glory?* (on tape) and that was apparently that.

Liam just looked so cool. Damon Albarn shared his matinee idol good looks, but seemed to carry the weight of the world on his shoulders. Liam, on the other hand, seemed confident and free, his message of "you've gotta love yourself mate, or no one else will love you," chiming perfectly with this particular insecure teenager.

Many Oasis' songs were sing-along anthems, and it was the likes of Wonderwall, Some Might Say, Live Forever and Don't Look Back in Anger that initially snared my interest. But as I began to explore their work, it was their more introspective side, more Noel's territory than Liam's, that helped funnel my alien feelings about the world.

A thought captured perfectly in Columbia from *Definitely Maybe* in 1994:

> *I can't tell you the way that I feel,*
> *Because the way I feel is oh so new to me*

With the release of box sets of the singles from the first two albums made up to look like packets of

Benson & Hedges cigarettes (you wouldn't get that now) in November 1996, there was suddenly a whole new world of material to discover. I quickly fell in love with Take Me Away, D'You Wanna be a Spaceman and Fade Away, initially drawn by the haunting melodies, but then captured by the yearning for escape from an oppressive world.

The world of *Definitely Maybe* gave way to that of *Morning Glory* and the story seemed to shift away from escape and focused instead on making a mark. Rock 'n' Roll Star, a song about dreaming of being on stage, made way for Don't Look Back in Anger, a song about making sure you don't mess up when you get there, and Champagne Supernova, its title imagining what the trappings of enormous success may well look like.

And then there was nothing new for sixteen months and I, like so many others, was left bereft. Recordings, videos and books were poured over again and again because, with no YouTube or Spotify, that was all there was. After obsessively reading the *NME* every week, waiting for an announcement of new music, it finally came in the form of the four track CD *D'You Know What I Mean*. The most eagerly awaited single of the year (perhaps of the nineties) broke the ice perfectly. It was an anthem for the people, bringing us all together in its chorus lyric: "All my people right here, right now; d'you know what I mean?"

Be Here Now was released on the day I opened the envelope containing my GCSE results. A strange coincidence considering bands almost always released albums on a Monday. Thursday 21st August 1997 is a date etched in my memory forever, partly because of my fair to middling grades, but chiefly because of the queue in Our Price that snaked out the door at 10am when everyone should have been at work. It wasn't just made up of stroppy teenagers but seemed to span all ages. It felt as if the whole of the UK briefly united in a moment, music holding it together. It echoed 2nd May, just three months earlier, when Tony Blair stepped into 10 Downing Street and a wave of positivity washed over the country; a wave that came to a crashing halt on 31st August when Princess Diana died in Paris and the country went into mourning.

Three years later, *Standing on the Shoulder of Giants* was released, but, for me, something had shifted. I still followed the release and bought the CD singles and album, but it no longer felt as important to me as it once did. Having said that, the year 2000 was also when I finally got to see Oasis play live, somewhat fittingly, at Reading Festival. The show was excellent, the band, with its new line-up, was on top form, and the key highlights were Noel telling the council to stick the fine for going over their allotted time on his platinum credit card, and an unscheduled light show of fork lightning during Wonderwall.

By the time *Heathen Chemistry* came out I was no longer paying much attention to Oasis. I listened to the songs on the radio, but was immersed in newer, more current groups, namely The Strokes, The White Stripes, Black Rebel Motorcycle Club and, closer to home, The Libertines and Manchester's own new wave: Doves, Badly Drawn Boy, and Elbow. Then *Don't Believe the Truth* came and went, and I didn't even hear the tracks on *Dig Out Your Soul* until long after they had been released. Although there was a crowd who still adored them, the band were long past their time in the cultural spotlight, which meant that even if you did listen to Oasis, you certainly didn't tell anyone. Just like listening to Coldplay.

When they finally split, it was no great surprise, but it did feel like an important era was over. Right up until the end, it had been comforting to know that Oasis were there, still playing and releasing records, even if I wasn't listening to them. They had become an ingrained part of the cultural landscape of Britain, like their heroes The Rolling Stones, The Kinks and Paul McCartney, still playing somewhere in the background.

Looking back, I can see it was important that they stopped playing when they did. They had probably gone as far as they could as Oasis, and Liam and Noel had produced as much as they could together. The weight of all those fights finally crushed the brothers' relationship. Once seemingly unbreakable, it was now fractured, perhaps beyond repair. What remained, however, was their strength of character, forged in northern steel, and the impact they had made on the cultural landscape of the UK and of British rock music.

The world is a better place for having Oasis' music in it. And that's all that really matters.

n.b. all songs written by Noel Gallagher, unless otherwise stated.

CHAPTER ONE
From Burnage, Half the World Away
(The Hacienda to King Tut's Wah Wah Hut)

> *You couldn't say that anyone that was ever in*
> *Oasis, me included, was the best in the world at*
> *anything. But when it all came together, we made*
> *people feel something that was indefinable … And*
> *people will never forget the way you made them feel.*
> Noel Gallagher, 2016

Oasis started out in the Manchester suburb of Burnage as The Rain. Taking their name from the John Lennon penned B-side to the 1966 Beatles' single Paperback Writer was something of controversial move at the time. The Beatles were not as universally adulated in the late eighties as they are today. After the shock of John Lennon's death in 1980 had faded, and Imagine was released for a second time, the world's biggest band were seen as yesterday's news in a decade that championed the new. But, for The Rain, it was The Beatles' music that drew them together, acknowledging their brilliance despite what might have been popular at the time.

As would soon become clear, much of Oasis' musical identity was based on their love of the Fab Four, and it could be argued that their championing of the Liverpudlian group, and the press' attempts to position them as the new Beatles, helped The Beatles, at least in part, reclaim their legendary status in the mid-nineties.

Today, Oasis are so synonymous with their Scouse heroes that in Danny Boyle's 2019 film *Yesterday*, Himesh Patel's Jack wakes from a coma to find he is the only person to remember The Beatles' music. After Googling Oasis, he discovers they never existed either.

The original band line-up consisted of Paul Arthurs on guitar and chief song writing duties, Paul McGuigan on bass, Tony McCarroll on drums and Chris Hutton on vocals. Arthurs soon became known both affectionately and derogatorily (as is the Mancunian way) as Bonehead, due to his premature hair loss, McGuigan became Guigsy, and Tony, well, he remained Tony. Hutton, however, didn't have time for a nickname as he soon had to make way for the brooding masculine force that was the 18-year-old Liam Gallagher.

Like football, music is part of the fabric of Manchester and, in 1991, it poured from every doorway, every pub, every club and, in the case of Factory Records, every former warehouse, or … factory. Following the birth of punk in 1977, Manchester had built a solid reputation as one of the UK's leading musical cities, from punk to new wave, a route that led music fans directly to Joy Division and The Buzzcocks, to The Smiths and The Stone Roses, and the act that rose from the ashes of Joy Division, Factory's key asset, New Order.

Factory cemented their role in Manchester's scene when they opened the Haçienda in 1982. Where many labels may have chosen to invest their royalties in a recording studio or in developing new talent, Factory chose to plough New Order's money into Britain's most notorious nightclub. After the success of their early club nights at the Russell Club, this tactic seemed to make sense. However, a combination of mismanagement and poor attendance meant the nightclub haemorrhaged money for the first six or seven years, eventually devouring £2 million of New Order's royalties. As Peter Hook, bassist and founder member of Joy Division and New Order, says in his book *The Haçienda: How Not to Run a Night Club*: "On the back of [New Order's] huge increase in popularity, we set off on our first big tour of the States. It was a success, the first one where we made any money.

We were ecstatic … Until we were told we had to sign it all immediately over to the Haçienda to bail it out."[i]

In 1989 New Order managed to turn the tide for the club when they released their fifth studio album *Technique*. The record melded indie-rock guitar lines with acid house dance beats and synthesisers, combining the traditional world of rock and the burgeoning world of dance. Suddenly there was a place for a mega club to house the growing masses excited by this new music.

One such fan was 22-year-old Noel Gallagher, then a roadie for Manchester indie band the Inspiral Carpets, who felt like he had found his spiritual home at the Haçienda. The club environment played a major part in the creation of the anthemic music that he penned for Oasis, the idea being to bring together the we-are-one-ness of the club with the solidarity of the football terraces and transplant them to the gig venue.

Drugs gave a synthesised feeling to the scene that surrounded the Haç. Everything felt heightened. But it wasn't high enough for Noel. As Mat Whitecross, director of *Supersonic*, the 2016 documentary about Oasis, told the author in November 2018:

> *Just prior to Oasis beginning, you had grunge, this phenomenon which was kind of aggressive and angsty and has a rage about it, but ultimately is kind of nihilistic and can only ever end in you blowing your brains out because it's like 'I hate myself and I want to die' … he [Noel] said, that's the message of grunge, you know I couldn't sign up to that, but I love the energy of it and I love the crowds.*
>
> *He said that he also simultaneously had the Haçienda and the euphoria of the house music, and he said that was kind of artificial because it was*

*fuelled by drugs. I mean it was formed by a
sort of coming together of people but it
wasn't a mass movement ... people were
really high and just wanted to have a good
time, there wasn't anything else, it was just
ultimately quite empty ... somehow we had
harnessed those two elements: the euphoria
and coming together of people; but it had this
kind of aggressive energy and rage to it.*

Acid house, the Haçienda and the people Noel
met there, had a profound effect on shaping his musicality.
He even chose a track by Haç DJ A Guy Called Gerald as
one of his Desert Island Discs on BBC Radio 4 in 2015.

Noel's idea was not a new one but, as he has gone
on to prove again and again, one of his greatest strengths
is to build on the work of others, popularising the message
and bringing it to the masses. As he says in (I Got) The
Fever, the long forgotten B-side to 1997 single Stand By
Me: "As I saw on the breeze, I can see the sons of those
who came before me, and it's got me on my knees."

Glasgow band and future Oasis label mates Primal
Scream won the annual Mercury Music Prize for best
British album in 1992 for *Screamadelica*. A year earlier, when
the band were making their third record, people assumed
they would follow the familiar route of the feedback-
drenched, Rolling Stones-flecked, garage rock made
popular five years earlier by The Jesus and Mary Chain
(Scream front man Bobby Gillespie was the Chain's stand
up drummer on their debut album *Psychocandy*). But then
Haçienda DJ and all-round musical visionary Andrew
Weatherall intervened and banned the band from the
studio for much of its creation.

Not playing on much of their own record proved
unpopular with the group, but it certainly did the trick.
Screamadelica melded indie-rock and acid house into an
ecstasy-soaked psychedelic trip through Britain's club land.

Incidentally, Primal Scream were signed by the same man who went on to discover Oasis in 1993, Alan McGee, childhood friend of Gillespie and the force behind one of the most exciting labels in the UK in the early nineties, Creation.

But Oasis' journey was far from simple. Back in early 1991, Noel was still a long way from being part of the group, and younger brother Liam did not share his brother's enthusiasm for acid house. He wanted to lift rock music out of the gutter and away from the dance clubs, putting bands back on the pedestal that the sixties and seventies had created for them. It was this attitude, combined with Noel's euphoric melding together of the different musical worlds, that would soon give the band their raison d'être.

Like Noel's, Liam's idea was not new. His main contemporary influence came in the form of another key band in the Manchester story, The Stone Roses. While Joy Division had taken punk and pushed it forward into the new wave, the Roses, fuelled by amphetamines and cider, propelled themselves back to the mod rival scene of the sixties, onto their scooters and into the Northern Soul clubs. It was in one of these clubs that sixties soul singer Geno Washington took a liking to Ian Brown and convinced him he needed to be a singer.

The Stone Roses took the musicality of the sixties, when bands wrote tight, simple pop songs for mass consumption, and married it with modernity, eventually using drum loops and samples to create their own style of nineties indie music. If there was a band Oasis owed their career to, it was these fellow sons of Manchester.

Rather than popping pills in the Haçienda, Liam preferred to watch live bands in traditional music venues like the Carousel Club (later named Manchester International), where he first saw The Stone Roses play in February 1988, when he was 15 years old. Liam was drawn by singer Ian Brown, who managed to embody the anti-pop star image of Morrissey from The Smiths and Shaun Ryder from the Happy Mondays, while simultaneously exuding a rock star swagger reminiscent of Roger Daltrey from The Who or Rod Stewart. He completely captivated his audience by simply being himself. Liam stood in the crowd taking it all in. Here was a young man from the same city (who wasn't Morrissey); why couldn't he do that too?

Coincidentally, Noel was at that very same Stone Roses gig at the Carousel Club – the same club where the Gallagher brothers' parents had met way back in 1965, when they were both new to Manchester and looking to find some friends.

Liam knew Bonehead and Guigsy, bonding with them over their shared love of The Beatles, and started hanging around with the band sometime in early 1991. Much to Hutton's ire, Liam started turning up to rehearsals and then soundchecks. Before long, Hutton was out and Liam was in. His first act as the group's new front man was to rechristen them Oasis.

A band's name is crucial. There are many terrible groups with great names, but very few great groups with terrible names. It's often the first thing people hear about a band, sometimes well before they hear any music, so it needs to capture in a simple word or phrase everything that people need to know about them.

Oasis was the perfect name for this band. First, it was simple, matter of fact, to the point, just like their music and their identity as a group of people. It also stood on its own, going against the trend for bands called 'The Somethings'. It was just one word; a word that indicated that they were "slightly out on our own," as Liam says in *Supersonic*. And, most importantly, the aptly named Oasis appeared like a break from the nothingness of the barren mainstream desert.

As soon as Liam took up song writing duties with Bonehead the band immediately began to sound like a proper group. Early tracks sounded suspiciously similar to The Stone Roses, Take Me, for example, owing a lot to I Wanna Be Adored. Liam also had something of a passing – not un-affected – resemblance to Brown so, when the band began to gig at the Boardwalk, they naturally attracted early comparisons to the Roses.

Meanwhile, Noel had been a roadie for the Inspiral Carpets since May 1988, after meeting their guitarist at – where else? – a Stone Roses concert. He initially auditioned to be their lead singer but lost out to Tom Hingley from Too Much Texas. Instead Noel opted to carry flight cases and tune guitars, following the band through the most commercially successful part of their career. After much championing from DJ John Peel, the band's debut album *Life* went to number 2 in the UK Official Albums Chart and took them around the world, with Noel in tow.

The Inspiral Carpets gig lasted for two years. It ended because the band found Noel difficult to work with (in other words, he never did anything). But it was during this time that Noel met Mark 'Coyley' Coyle, who would go on to become Oasis' live sound engineer and one of their closest associates. The man who gave Oasis the huge live sound that captured the attention of Alan McGee was eventually forced to leave their inner circle when his hearing began to suffer in 1995.

Noel and Coyley were both members of what Noel later called the Manchester 50. A group of 50+ figures who attended every gig in town. Another member of the Manchester 50 was musician and music writer John Robb who remember Noel as "very shy, sort of young, 'cos we're all older. But he was definitely part of the scene."

Many felt that by the time that Oasis came along the scene in Manchester was over and it was London's turn again. As Robb told the author in 2018:

Well, I think it was funny with Oasis because in many ways they were the last of those Manchester bands to make it, you know? … they were definitely not invited to the party, and I think you always have to hand it to Alan McGee, for, well, inviting them to the party… no-one else was interested in them.

It was like, when they came out, to people in London, they would say 'There's no way another band is gonna come out of Manchester, you've had your turn!' London always has bands, and everybody else gets a 'scene', you know, 'the scene', 'the Manchester scene', 'the Liverpool scene', you get your little turn to be successful and then it goes back to the big city.

But Manchester broke that mould, you know, because it just kept having one band after another. But, Oasis were seen as being really really old fashioned and really out of step with the times, and what Noel says is, he says, 'The London music business set the stage for Blur, and then we turned up and they never forgave us.'

But, more on that later. For now, let's head back to Burnage.

Burnage is a suburb about twenty minutes to the south-east of central Manchester. Factory Records had links to most of Manchester's suburbs; in Burnage that link was Stockholm Monsters, a band on their roster between 1981 and 1987 whose debut single Fairy Tales reached number 43 in the UK independent charts in September 1981 (so not exactly what you might call a hit).

A young Noel Gallagher knew the group, and recognised that the route to forming a band could start on your own doorstep. "They were the first band ever to come from Burnage," he said, "And I think they had a hit with a song called Fairy Tales. From that you get to Joy Division, New Order and then it was The Smiths and then the Roses and then the Mondays, and then you start your own band."[ii]

The Golden Age

Noel and Liam's parents, Peggy and Tommy, had separately emigrated to Manchester from Ireland in 1965 in search of work, like so many young Irish citizens had done for nearly a hundred years. They were married not long after and their first child Paul came along in 1966, with Noel following in 1967, just as the city entered a new chapter as a "dark and dreary purgatory"[iii], totally at odds with its Victorian golden age. Liam was born in September 1972 as the city (and much of the North West) began to enter a deep recession. In the course of a little under 100 years, Manchester went from being the world's first industrialised city to being one of the first post-industrialised.

Like all the countries, cities and towns in which punk made the biggest impact, Manchester was predominantly made up of working-class families, many of whom had flooded into the city during the Industrial Revolution, expanding the population at an incredible and unsustainable rate. The latter half of the nineteenth century was the city's so-called golden age, and for many years it was the centre of the world's textile manufacturing industry. Cotton produced in the numerous local mills manned by people drawn from all over the country was boxed up and sent down the network of canals to Liverpool, where it was shipped around the Empire. In Australia, New Zealand and South Africa, sheets, pillowcases and all manner of bedding are still called 'Manchester' to this day.

The system was so successful that Manchester became famous the world over as the first fully industrialised city, ahead of the vast metropolises of London and New York.

Manchester was hit hard in the Second World War, its production of bombs and Lancaster bombers making it an obvious target for the Luftwaffe. But, post-war, the textile industry continued to dominate, and more and more immigrants from Ireland and the dwindling British Empire, notably India, poured into the city in search of work. The city continued to grow and, by 1963, it had the country's third largest port, which is incredible considering that it is fifty miles from the nearest coastline. Much of the working-class population relied on the cotton mills and the support infrastructure that grew up around the industry, such as butchers and bakers, for work. The archaic canal system could no longer support the demand for textiles or the growing size of the container ships, and by 1968 the cotton exchange closed, a victim of its own success. The port clung on but was eventually closed under Margaret Thatcher's regime of tyrannical austerity in 1982.

Between 1961 and 1982, 150,000 jobs were lost in the manufacturing industry in Manchester, forcing the city's working-class population to seek alternative employment at a time when jobs were increasingly scarce. It was revealed in 2011 under the thirty-year rule that Thatcher was urged to abandon Liverpool to "managed decline"[iv] after the notorious Toxteth riots in 1981, which came about, just like the Brixton riots a year earlier, due to a long-standing clash between the police and the black community. The unrest highlighted just how desperate things had become in the North West after the decline of the manufacturing industry.

Manchester "felt like a piece of history that had been spat out"[v]. Rows of Victorian houses built for the once vital working populace gave way to streets of rubble shaped by the Luftwaffe, which were, in turn, replaced by huge blocks of flats, concrete fortresses, futuristic and Stalinist. The town planners "did more damage to Manchester than the German bombers"[vi], said Frank Owen from indie band Manicured Noise. If the late nineteenth century was Manchester's golden age, then the early 1970s were its antithesis. The cotton trade lost, unemployment spread like a disease. Groups with time on their hands began to congregate and bands started to form. Young people had something to rebel against, and punk gave them the means to do it.

Fast forward to the early nineties and 24-year-old Noel Gallagher was working on a building site. His tradesman father had found him his first building job when he was 18 – the first contact he'd had with his son since they'd become estranged ten years earlier.

Peggy and her three sons were all victims of Tommy's violent temper but, for some reason, it was Noel who bore the brunt. It continued for many years, until Peggy finally managed to arrange other accommodation and they left. Tommy made no attempt to find them and it was pure chance that reunited Noel with his father. He helped him find work in the building sector, but once Noel could find his own work, contact ceased again. It would be a further three years and several million records sold before the Gallagher brothers would see their father again.

Noel suffered a leg injury working on the building site that meant he was confined to the storeroom. Bored with the quiet, he began bringing his guitar to work, composing much of what would become *Definitely Maybe*, including the future classic Live Forever.

Meanwhile, Liam and Oasis were still rehearsing and gigging. At his little brother's insistence, Noel went along to one of the gigs at the Boardwalk. It was not a life changing concert. The band had only the most rudimentary of musical ability, but as a frontman, Liam clearly had something, and Noel liked that they wrote their own songs. Liam asked his brother to be their manager, mainly because of his contacts with the Inspiral Carpets, but Noel laughed away the offer. Eventually, however, he came down to the rehearsal room with his guitar to jam. Liam had heard him play the future number 1 single All Around the World in the bedroom they shared and urged him to play it for the others.

Oasis with Noel as lead guitarist had their first official gig at the Broadwalk on 14th August 1991[vii]. Considering how this story eventually played out, it was something of an anti-climax. As Noel says in *Supersonic*: "Then it went nowhere for two years. We had nothing written about us. No one even said we were shit!" The band continued to play in the North West, mostly in Manchester and mostly at the Broadwalk (where they also rehearsed), with a couple of treks to Liverpool and London.

They also recorded their first demo tape, which would later become known as *Live Demonstration* (original copies now exchange hands for several thousand pound). Recorded between March and May 1993 at Porter Street Studios in Liverpool, *Live Demonstration* made it into the hands of Alan McGee after the band impressed him at King Tut's in Glasgow.

The studio was owned by Tony Griffiths from Liverpool band The Real People, who Noel had met while touring with the Inspiral Carpets in America, and who would eventually record backing vocals for Oasis' debut single Supersonic, credited as Anthony Griffiths, a year later.

Consisting of several tracks that ended up either on *Definitely Maybe* or as B-sides to the band's early singles, songs recorded in the sessions included: Cloudburst (B-side to Live Forever), Rock 'n' Roll Star (opening track on *Definitely Maybe*), Bring it on Down (*Definitely Maybe*),

Columbia (*Definitely Maybe*, and the group's first white label release), Alive (B-side to Supersonic), and Fade Away (B-side to Cigarettes and Alcohol).

Also included in the sessions were four songs recorded live in rehearsal but which for whatever reason, dropped out of the Oasis catalogue, later finding their way in chunks onto later compositions. Must be the Music is now all but forgotten, but Lock all the Doors was later reworked into a version released on Noel's second solo album *Chasing Yesterday* in 2015. Strange Thing, one of the band's earliest songs, consisted of a riff incredibly similar to the yet to be released Stone Roses' 1994 number 2 single Love Spreads, and was the only one of these songs to be included on the track listing of the demo tape. Perhaps most interestingly, Noel later recycled much of Comin' on Strong as the basis of his vocal on the first of his Chemical Brothers collaborations, Setting Sun, which made it to number 1 in October 1996.

The demo also included two acoustic tracks recorded in Mark Coyle's bedroom before the band were signed, and which were officially released without being rerecorded. Married with Children was the final track on *Definitely Maybe*, and acoustic live favourite D'You Wanna Be a Spaceman, sung by Noel, ended up as the B-side to second single Shakermaker.

The demo cover image with the now famous Union Jack flag swirling down a plughole, was designed by Tony French, another friend of Noel's. In 1993, the tape was passed around with various track listings. In 2014, it was released properly in a mega-limited new format, designed to look exactly like the original, remastered by Mark Coyle as part of the band's twentieth anniversary celebrations.

The reissued demo included the following track listing:

Side One:
1. Cloudburst
2. Columbia
3. D'You Wanna be a Spaceman
4. Strange Thing

Side Two:
1. Bring it on Down
2. Married with Children
3. Fade Away
4. Rock n Roll Star

Factory's City

Around the same time that Oasis were beginning to gig around Manchester, the 15-year dominance of the city's leading independent label Factory Records was coming to an end. Frankly, it was amazing the label had lasted as long as it had, considering the colossal amount of money they had burnt through. And as John Robb pointed out, the feeling was spreading through Manchester that something was over.

Aside from the Haçienda, which was subsidised by New Order, Factory spent around a quarter of a million pounds on recording the debut album by Peter Hook's side-project Revenge, even though it was recorded in his own commercial studio, Suite 16. They also spent upwards of £700,000 refurbishing their former textile factory headquarters on Charles Street, which included the infamous floating table, which alone cost £20,000.[viii]

Taking its name from the New York nightclub which itself owed a debt to the pop art movement spearheaded by Andy Warhol, Factory was founded by company directors Tony Wilson, Alan Erasmus, Rob

Gretton (Joy Division/New Order manager), Martin Hannett (producer) and Peter Saville (graphic designer). All five took an equal share and had an equal say. The idea was simple: to expose Manchester bands to a national audience on their own terms – something they would not be afforded if they signed to a major label. Factory covered the costs of recording and, after those costs were recouped (they rarely were), all the profits were split 50:50 between band and label.

As well as Joy Division/New Order, Factory's position in the Manchester music scene in the late seventies provided an elevated launch pad for North West bands looking for more exposure than your average indie label could offer. These included eighties synth-pop pioneers Orchestral Manoeuvres in the Dark and fey indie-icons James. Factory recorded and released singles that these acts could then use to court major labels. This seemingly altruistic attitude was typical of Factory's approach to releasing music. For them, it was all about the power of the songs, rather than their commercial value. What they didn't seem to realise was that a label needs to make money to survive.

No Manchester band could avoid Factory, so it was with a certain inevitability that Oasis tried to sign with them in 1992. "Before Creation, we only ever went to one label, and that was Factory," said Noel Gallagher in *Shadowplayers*[ix]. Factory A&R Phil Saxe wanted to sign them, even though many in Manchester thought they were too similar to The Stone Roses. But as he explained in *Shadowplayers*: "We couldn't have signed them, to be fair. We wouldn't have had the money to promote them." At the time, Factory owed something like £2 million and, by November 1992, was declared bankrupt. Their back catalogue was bought by London Records, a stinging insult from one of the major metropolitan city labels they had tried so hard to stand against.

So Factory's loss became Creation's gain.

Creation Records was run like a business, seeking those all-important chart positions while trying to honour their indie roots. With Oasis they found the perfect band to straddle these two positions.

Creation was founded by Alan McGee, Dick Green and Joe Foster in 1983, and their earliest signings included the Jesus and Mary Chain, Primal Scream, My Bloody Valentine and Ride. Their first release was the 7" single, '73 in '83 by The Legend, which McGee funded with a £1,000 bank loan.

A year later, the label had its first commercial success with the Jesus and Mary Chain's first single Upside Down, but it wasn't until 1990 that things really heated up when both Primal Scream and Ride produced top 40 singles, and Ride's debut album *Nowhere* made the top 20. After this, the label went from strength to strength and, in 1991, Primal Scream released their Mercury Prize-winning *Screamadelica*, Teenage Fanclub put out *Bandwagonesque* and My Bloody Valentine released the classic *Loveless*. In 1992, Ride's single, Leave Them All Behind, made the top 10 and McGee sold Sony almost half the shares in the label, gaining access to worldwide distribution while retaining creative control.

McGee stumbled across Oasis at King Tut's Wah Wah Hut in Glasgow on 31st May 1993. As a Glaswegian, he was aware of the venue's reputation and so, having just missed his train back to London after visiting his sister, thought he would pop in to see his ex-girlfriend Debbie Reynolds' band The Sister Lovers. Oasis thought they were booked to play on the same bill, but on showing up were told "no chance" by the promoter as he already had three bands booked. Legend has it that Noel, Oasis and a dozen mates they had brought with them threatened to smash the place up if he didn't let them on. After considering his options, the promoter squeezed them in. Reynolds claims she offered to share her band's slot, so

Oasis were able to play without resorting to violence. But a good story is a good story.

Oasis played for twenty minutes, and that was all the time that McGee needed to know he was going to sign them. Mark Coyle knew McGee from his days engineering for Creation band The Boo Radleys. Acting as go-between, he introduced McGee to Noel, and the rest is history. Or nearly.

Not long before the Glasgow gig, Noel had been leaving HMV in Manchester when he bumped into an acquaintance from the Haçienda. People who went to the Haç tended to make friends, such was the loved-up-ness of the place, but it was rare that they stayed in touch outside of the hallowed walls. However, Ian stopped to ask Noel what he had bought. "The The's new album, *Solitude*," said Noel. "Oh, that's our kid's band," replied Ian. It transpired that Ian was Ian Maher, younger brother of John Maher, or Johnny Marr as he was known on stage as former guitarist with The Smiths and current guitarist with The The.

In his autobiography, Marr talks about his brother giving him a copy of the *Live Demonstration* demo. "What I heard sounded new yet immediately familiar in a good way," he said, " … it was flying the flag for classic rock but had a thing of its own, and there wasn't anything else like it. It was so … Manchester."[x]

He also remembers meeting Liam for the first time at Noel's flat: "I was introduced to a young kid sitting on the couch with an amazing haircut … who was flanked by two pretty young girls so enthralled by him and his hair that they didn't seem to notice anyone entering the tiny flat."

Johnny introduced Noel to his manager and head of Ignition Management Marcus Russell, who signed Oasis up after the King Tuts concert. By early June, Noel, Liam and Bonehead were on a train from Manchester Piccadilly to London Euston and on to 83 Clerkenwell

Road to sign on the dotted line. The train broke down en route and Noel composed a new song while they waited. Going Nowhere, one of his finest early compositions, ended up as the B-side to Stand by Me in October 1997.

It's easy to see where his head was at when writing the lyric:

> *Gonna get me a motor car,*
> *Maybe a Jaguar,*
> *Maybe a plane or a day away,*
> *Gonna be a millionaire,*
> *So can you take me,*
> *Wanna be wild 'cause my life's so tame,*
> *Here am I, going nowhere on a train.*

For Noel, it seemed his nowhere days were behind him. He had turned 26 a week earlier. Liam was just 21.

CHAPTER TWO
Creation, Supersonic and _Definitely Maybe_ (1993-1994)

Sony Music bought nearly 50% of Creation Records in 1992, giving Alan McGee a much larger worldwide distribution network, plus the fairly agreeable upfront sum of £2 million, some of which could be spent on recording and promoting his brand-new signing.

What it meant in real terms, however, was that he still had the power to sign whichever artists he liked, but now had to answer to a board of trustees, none of whom cared about music as much as they did profit. This was a million miles away from Factory's fly-by-the-seat-of-your-pants approach that spurned artistic oppression in favour of total creative freedom. Luckily for McGee, the new band he was taking a punt on was about to become one of the most successful British groups of all time.

The deal also meant that Oasis were only signed to Creation in the UK and Ireland; for the rest of the world they were represented by Sony's subsidiary Epic, and so subject to whatever release schedule the bods there wished to follow. In America, Epic chose to release Rock 'n' Roll Star, Morning Glory and Champagne Supernova as singles, none of which were released in the UK. Noel's instinct to take on a manager before signing the deal was, therefore, a wise one, and with Marcus Russell they couldn't really have asked for anyone better to handle their business affairs. After Alan McGee, Russell is probably the most important non-musician in the Oasis story.

Noel had learned from the mistakes The Stone Roses had made. Their manager, Gareth Evans, signed a deal with Silvertone Records in 1988 that was so bad for the band that, amongst other things, they made no money from CD sales, only vinyl, just at the time when CDs were taking over as the main format for music distribution. When the inevitable split came, it was so bitterly acrimonious that a court ruling prevented the band from releasing any new music for four years. Although the band came back fighting with the *Second Coming* album in 1994, the damage done to the momentum they had created was lost and into the hole they left stepped Oasis.

Russell, who in his previous life as a sometime promoter had put a concert by The Sex Pistols whilst at university, worked with Oasis until they split in 2009. After that he managed Beady Eye, and Noel Gallagher's High Flying Birds. After Creation folded in 1999, he became managing director of the newly founded Big Brother Recordings, the label created to release Oasis' records, and which he still runs today.

In the early days of Oasis' success, Russell was running Ignition from his flat and answering the phone himself (assisted by Marr, who was also based there a lot of the time). But their speedy ascension meant Russell needed to relocate and soon had an office in Lindhope Street, just round the corner from Baker Street in North London, where The Beatles' Apple Records was based. Ignition are still there today.

Putting Russell in touch with the band was only the first of three major favours that Johnny Marr offered the group as they were taking off. The second was gifting Noel the sunburst finish Les Paul Standard guitar that can be seen on the cover of the group's first single, Supersonic. And the third was putting them in touch with his engineer Owen Morris, who had access to Marr's studio and used it to save *Definitely Maybe* from the scrap heap.

As Marr recounts in his autobiography *Set the Boy Free*, Noel called him up distraught after the guitar came into contact with a stage invader's head at a gig in

Newcastle. With typical generosity, Marr packaged up another Les Paul guitar and couriered it up to Noel for the band's next gig. And this wasn't just any guitar – it was a gift from Pete Townsend of The Who, meaning there was a beautiful rock lineage at play as the guitar was handed from one generation to the next. Nice one Johnny.

Creation and Russell's first move was to get the newly signed band playing live as often as possible. By September, they were playing Manchester, Sheffield, Leeds, Birmingham and London, with a white label of Columbia doing the rounds of the DJ circuit.

This version of Columbia was recorded at Porter Street Studios earlier in 1993, and differs from the final version that made it onto *Definitely Maybe* in a few key ways. There is a sample at the top end of the recording, a looped indecipherable voice that could be Liam's, before the song kicks in proper. There is also a sample at the end of a chanting female voice looping round and round, baring something of a similarity to the samples used in I Am the Walrus.

As is to be expected from a demo, the guitars don't sound as full as they would on the album, but there is nothing lacking in Liam's self-assured vocal delivery, which was probably what prompted the band to release the song to DJs in an effort to drum up some early support. Perhaps most notably, Noel doesn't sing on the song. In fact, he gave very few backing performances until they recorded the album proper, leaving Liam to harmonise with himself on the song's chorus.

Otherwise, the song's components are all in place and it's the driving simplicity of the track – just A, D and C barre chords and a simple looped guitar riff – that makes it so listenable. The song takes its name from the Columbia Hotel in London's Hyde Park where the band often stayed in the early days. Perhaps not surprisingly, they were eventually barred. Fittingly, the band opened their era defining concerts at Knebworth with Columbia, linking their peak with their beginning.

Single 1:

Supersonic
Released: 11th April 1994; UK Chart Position: 31;
Label: Creation; Album: *Definitely Maybe*
B-sides: Take Me Away; I Will Believe; Columbia
(White Label)
Producer: Mark Coyle

By December 1993 it was time for Oasis to record their first single and Alan McGee was keen to release Bring it on Down, one of the faster, punkier tracks from *Definitely Maybe*. At the recording session though, Noel snuck off during dinner and wrote Supersonic in half an hour. He then played it down the phone to McGee, who threatened to sack all the other bands on the label for not being as talented as his new signing, and with his blessing, the band side-lined Bring it on Down and recorded Supersonic that night, the freshness of the new song complimenting the guttural punk rock DIY sound.

Supersonic was the perfect song to bring the band to the main stage. Beginning with a simple, four-to-the-floor McCarroll drum beat and an immediately distinctive Noel guitar intro, the song then launches into the Bonehead and Guigsy led barre chord riff of F#m, A and B, sounding not a million miles away from the likes of Nirvana and the American grunge bands. Totally at odds with the negativity of those bands though, Liam's snarly vocal bursts into life with the opening line: "I need to be myself, I can be no one else." Oasis had arrived.

Released on 11th April 1994, the song reached a respectable number 31 in the UK Official Singles Chart, where it hung around for four weeks before disappearing and then reappearing on and off in the top 100 over the following months. As the band's popularity began to gather momentum in 1995 and 1996, the song, along with all of Oasis' early singles, enjoyed another lease of life.

Supersonic had a notable 30 week run in the bottom reaches of the top 100 between 11th November 1995 and 1st June 1996. This was as a result of the tandem release of the Benson & Hedges-style singles box sets of their first two albums, released on 5th November 1995 and 11th November 1995 respectively.

Despite being the band's lowest charting single, by 2019 Supersonic had sold more copies, some 250,000, than many of the band's number 1 singles, including The Hindu Times, Lyla and The Importance of Being Idle.

Although the cover of the single featured the band in Monnow Valley Studio in South Wales (where they recorded *Definitely Maybe*), the song was recorded in The Pink Museum in Liverpool, and produced by their old friend Mark Coyle.

Noel didn't provide backing vocals on the A-side, but was the sole performer on the first B-side, Take Me Away, a heartfelt acoustic ballad about wanting to escape from whatever it is that holds you trapped (in Noel's case: Manchester).

The song, which began the trend for Noel taking over the lead vocal on standard acoustic ballads, could not be more at odds with the A-side, except perhaps for the drug references, of which – surprisingly for such a delicate song – there are two: "Me and my soul we know where we're going, we'll go where the grass is free and the air is clean," and "You could be me and pretty soon you will be, but you're gonna need a line."

UK Official Singles Chart – Top 10 – 17ᵗʰ April 1994:

1. The Most Beautiful Girl in the World – Symbol (Prince)
2. Everything Changes – Take That
3. The Real Thing – Tony Di Bart
4. Always – Erasure
5. Mmm mmm mmm mmm – Crash Test Dummies
6. Streets of Philadelphia – Bruce Springsteen
7. Like to Move It – Reel 2 Real ft. Mad Stuntman
8. Dedicated to the One I Love – Bitty McLean
9. Rock My Heart – Haddaway
10. The Sign – Ace of Base

………………………..

31. Supersonic – Oasis

The singles chart the week of the release of Supersonic showed a post-grunge, pre-Britpop world largely bereft of guitar music. Straightforward pop had a strong hold, which tends to be the case between major musical movements. In this top 10 we can see light rock in the form of Crash Test Dummies, and a Bruce Springsteen song taken from the Oscar-winning film *Philadelphia* (1992) starring Tom Hanks, while Dedicated to the One I Love comes from the reggae revival of the early nineties. In the remainder of the top 100, only Blur, Pulp and Paul Weller offer the slightest hint of the music just around the corner.

Those with a keen eye for dates will notice that the single was released on 11ᵗʰ April 1994, just six days after Kurt Cobain died. That's how quickly music can change. Grunge was all but over and British rock music was being ushered into a new era.

The Death of Grunge

Cobain's death provided a symbolic end point for grunge and made the acts that had been there at the beginning take a look at the beast they had created: corporate grunge. Record companies, looking to capitalise on Nirvana shifting five million copies of *Nevermind*, made commodities out of groups singing about despair and self-hatred, hawking them like cheap cars.

Billy Corgan and the Smashing Pumpkins, riding the wave of success of their second album *Siamese Dream*, were all too happy to play along. despite the retrospective classic status awarded to their 1995 third album *Mellon Collie and the Infinite Sadness*, its overly long 28-track list and musical eclecticism pushed the band toward bloated musical pretension, and gave Corgan an air of arrogance, from which he and the band never fully recovered.

Similarly, Soundgarden, who had a huge hit with their album *Superunknown* in 1994, toured Europe as part of a bill of six bands (White Zombie, Pennywise, Blind Melon, Mudhoney and Britain's own Reef) throughout 1995, neatly wrapped up in a ready-to-rent festival tour package. Mudhoney, one of the premier grunge acts, said the package was "probably the six most horrible bands in the world at that time".[xi]

Pearl Jam, who had mainstreamed the grunge movement alongside Nirvana, refused to make music videos in 1994, fearing they had become the exact thing they were rebelling against; the Pixies split after an ill-advised tour supporting U2 in 1993; and Cobain's widow Courtney Love, at the centre of the maelstrom, had a nervous breakdown on stage with her band Hole at Reading Festival in August 1994.

Four years later, Love and her band returned, sparkly clean and playing the game, with *Celebrity Skin*. The album was a corporate grunge dream, with clear cut distorted guitars and songs thematically centred on

California and Los Angeles. The band's original drummer was forced to make way for a session musician who could drum in time, and perhaps most pertinently, nearly half of the tracks were co-written by Billy Corgan.

Damon Albarn from Blur wanted to kill off grunge with the band's second album *Modern Life is Rubbish* in 1993 to make space for British bands. By the end of 1994, British bands were becoming increasingly popular, thanks predominantly to Blur's *Parklife* and to Pulp's *His 'n' Hers*, which reached number 9 at the end of April. Musical movements rise and fall with the tide, and it seemed that grunge was on its way out, just in time for Oasis' debut album.

By 1996, Blur were joined not only by Oasis, but by Pulp, Ocean Colour Scene, Paul Weller, The Cranberries and Supergrass, all with million selling albums.

Single 2:

Shakermaker
Released: 13th June 1994; UK Chart Position: 11; Label: Creation; Album: *Definitely Maybe*
B-sides: D'You Wanna Be a Spaceman; Alive; Bring it on Down (Live)
Producers: Mark Coyle, Owen Morris, Noel Gallagher

Oasis' first *NME* cover was on 4th June 1994, a week before the release of their second single Shakermaker. The band were already beginning to make a name for themselves not only for their music, but for their rock 'n' roll behaviour and hedonistic, party boy antics. An uncharacteristically tranquil Liam appeared on the cover beneath a sign for The Oasis Bar, alongside the headline: "Totally Cool". Under the words "Those Windows are Saying Throw A Chair Through Me", the article inside follows the band through a series of post-gig hotel bars, stealing, downing beer, champagne and anything alcoholic, abusing boyband East 17, and generally causing the mayhem that would soon come to define their off-stage life.

What is reassuring about the article is that the band appear just as they do when they are at the peak of their fame three years later. Their drunken antics are augmented by the Gallagher brothers' constant squabbling, their love of football (in particular Manchester City) and the music of The Beatles, all of which define them as a band. This group of young lads were in no way contrived; fame didn't change them, it just enhanced their behaviour, perhaps made it more acceptable, and certainly more obvious to the general public. But then, if you've sold a million records, more people take notice if you steal thirty bottles of beer when the bartender isn't looking.

Shakermaker was a bold choice for a second single and the fact that it reached number 11 perhaps says a lot more about the growing popularity of the band than it does the strength of the song. The track is a mid-tempo number based on a simple twelve bar blues formation in B7, and it owes a debt to mid-late Beatles, notably I Am the Walrus (nonsensical psychedelic lyrics) and Flying from the *Magical Mystery Tour* EP (music).

The melody also shares more than a passing resemblance to the New Seekers 1972 Coca-Cola ode to world peace, I'd Like to Teach the World to Sing. The copyright owners may well have never noticed the similarity had Liam not developed a penchant for singing the lyrics to the Coke ad version ("I'd like to buy the world a Coke") instead of Noel's. The case was settled out of court, eating up a chunk of the band's yet to be earned royalties.

Similar to its predecessor, the single initially had a five-week run on the charts, before dropping in and out of the top 100, experiencing its longest run from 27th January to 25th May 1996, after the box sets were released. The B-sides were D'You Wanna Be a Spaceman?, another Noel-led acoustic number about the dreams of childhood fading away as real life responsibilities begin to pile up, Alive, another demo from the Real People studio sessions and a live version of Bring it On Down.

UK Official Singles Chart – Top 10 – 26th June 1994:

1. Love is All Around – Wet Wet Wet
2. I Swear – All-4-One
3. Swamp Thing – Grid
4. Baby I Love Your Way – Big Mountain
5. You Don't Love Me (No, No, No) – Dawn Penn
6. Don't Turn Around – Ace of Base
7. Go On Move – Reel 2 Real ft. Mad Stuntman
8. No Good (Start the Dance) – Prodigy
9. Shine – Aswad
10. U & Me – Cappella
   ....
11. Shakermaker – Oasis

The singles chart the week that Shakermaker peaked at number 11 shows pop was once again the genre of choice, with grunge on its way out and Britpop yet to take hold. Wet Wet Wet were at number 1 with their mega-hit Love is All Around from the film *Four Weddings and a Funeral*, the surprise hit of 1994, if not the decade. The single spent 15 weeks at number 1, the joint longest run in the top spot alongside Bryan Adams' (Everything I Do) I Do it for You, also taken from a film soundtrack, this time *Robin Hood, Prince of Thieves* (1991).

If you glance further down the chart, however, you discover some early singles by both current and future Britpop favourites. Shed Seven were at number 28 with their second single Dolphin; Echobelly were at number 38 with their third single I Can't Imagine the World Without Me; Blur were at number 46 with To The End (the final single from *Parklife*); and Madchester survivors The Charlatans were at 48 with Jesus Hairdo.

A pre-Britpop Manic Street Preachers were also at number 87 with Faster (the first single from their opus album *The Holy Bible*); Strangelove were at 88 with Time For the Rest of Your Life; and Pulp's breakthrough single The Sisters EP, which had peaked at 19 five weeks earlier and featured the classic song Babies, was just clinging on at number 100.

Single 3:

Live Forever
Released: 8th August 1994; UK Chart Position: 10;
Label: Creation; Album: *Definitely Maybe*
B-sides: Up in the Sky (acoustic); Cloudburst;
Supersonic (live)
Producers: Mark Coyle, Owen Morris, Noel Gallagher

Clearly unable to keep it under wraps any longer and wait the requisite three months for the band's next single, Live Forever was released into the world on 8th August 1994, three weeks before *Definitely Maybe*. Building on the band's rolling success, it was their first single to dent the top 10, peaking at number 10. It went on to spend 68 weeks on the chart, appearing in the top 50 as recently as June 2017.

Live Forever is one of the most important songs of the nineties, and the song that made Noel realise that there might be something special about his song writing ability. "I knew enough about songs and about music," he says in *Supersonic*, "to know that was a great song. And then one followed another."

Recorded at Sawmills at the same time as the rest of what would eventually become *Definitely Maybe*, the echo-drenched layers of guitars hark back to the recently passed shoegazing bands such as label mates Ride, or The Stone Roses classic debut LP, linking the song to a time and place, while the lyrics distil the growing optimism in Britain. The negativity of grunge was no longer in vogue, and as Britain was slowly finding its way out of another recession, people wanted something to feel positive about. Live Forever provided that release.

> *Maybe I just wanna fly*
> *Wanna live, I don't wanna die*
> *Maybe I just wanna breathe*
> *Maybe I just don't believe*
> *Maybe you're the same as me*
> *We see things they'll never see*
> *You and I we're gonna live forever*

Live Forever is a working class hymn every bit as important as A Design for Life by Manic Street Preachers. It borrows the ethereal metaphors of another working-class hero, John Lennon, most notably during his Imagine period in the years immediately post-Beatles. Imagine was a literary image Lennon borrowed from Yoko Ono, who wrote in 1963, "Imagine the clouds dripping, dig a hole in your garden to put them in". Noel mixes Lennon and Ono's abstract delivery with his own sense of reality, allowing the listener to find their own sense of freedom through the song. By using words such as 'fly' and 'breathe', Noel evokes the feeling of escaping from where and when we are born and, as the title suggests, perhaps even escaping death.

The Lennon connection marries the arty sixties optimism and the gritty man-on-the-street northern realism that clung to Oasis as their legend began to gather momentum in 1994. The press wanted the band to be the

Sex Pistols, but Live Forever gave them an identity beyond the classic nihilism of punk and the bleak imagery of post-punk. The nineties was not a bleak period. People had survived the long periods of unemployment, limited housing and heavy-handed bureaucracy that were so prevalent in the late seventies and eighties, and with Tony Blair taking over as leader of the Labour party in 1994, there was a very real opportunity for change on the horizon.

The second part of the chorus invites the listener to join Noel and the band in the imaginary world created by the song, in the same way that the final lines of Imagine do:

> Live Forever:
> *Maybe you're the same as me*
> *We see things they'll never see*
> *You and I we're gonna live forever*

> Imagine:
> *You may say I'm a dreamer*
> *But I'm not the only one*
> *I hope someday you'll join us*
> *And the world will be as one*

Noel's lyrics reflect the we-are-one-ness he experienced at the Haçienda, swapping the artificiality of drugs for something real, just as Oasis favoured acoustic instruments over synthesisers and digitally created music. There was an honesty to their music that built on the idea of the audience as an extension of the band, just like a football team's supporters are an extension of the team themselves. And for Oasis and their fans, Live Forever was the team anthem.

The penultimate line of the chorus ("we see things they'll never see") further fuels the football team analogy by creating an us and them, the idea of an opposing force to rally against helping to bolster the strength of the home team. This also supports the anthemic working-class nature of the song: together we are more powerful. Just as football hooliganism led to atrocious levels of violence in the eighties in the UK and in mainland Europe, the idea of following a band like a team resulted in unnecessary animosity. The Battle of Britpop in 1995 saw Oasis and Blur go head to head in the charts, pushing Britpop into the mainstream, but also building tension and negative rivalry.

Two groups competing for the title of Britain's best band was not new, but back in the sixties The Beatles and the Rolling Stones were good friends, guesting on each other's records. The Beatles even included "Welcome the Rolling Stones" on the cover of *Sgt. Pepper's Lonely Hearts Club Band* in 1967, emblazoned on the jumper of a teddy bear. It was The Beatles *and* the Rolling Stones, just like it was The Stone Roses *and* the Happy Mondays in 1990. In 1995, however, it was Oasis versus Blur. Indeed, this was precisely what the coverline said on the *NME* on 12th August 1995, two days before the release of the two singles.

UK Official Singles Chart – Top 10 – 14th August 1994:

1. Love is All Around – Wet Wet Wet
2. Crazy for You – Let Loose
3. I Swear – All-4-One
4. Searching – China Black
5. Compliments on Your Kiss – Red Dragon with Brian and Tony
6. What's Up – DJ Miko
7. Regulate – Warren G & Nate Dogg
8. 7 Seconds – Youssou N'Dour ft. Neneh Cherry
9. (Meet) The Flintstones – BC-52s
10. **Live Forever – Oasis**

Straightforward pop music was still the order of the day as summer marched on in 1994, with Wet Wet Wet's reign at the top of the charts marking pop music's dominance. The reggae revival was making itself known in the form of Compliments on Your Kiss, while songs from films were also still popular, with (Meet) The Flintstones, the theme tune to the ill-advised live action remake of the classic cartoon performed by the B-52s (who changed their name to the BC-52s specially for the occasion) joining Love is All Around in the top 10 .

Other singles of note in the chart that week were Haçienda and Boardwalk DJs 808 State at 85 with Bombadin; trip-hop Bristol outfit Portishead at 79 with Sour Times (down from 13); Everything but the Girl at 69 with Missing (which would reach number 3 on its rerelease in October); and the pop-punk classic Basket Case by Green Day at number 55 (this was also rereleased in January 1995, reaching number 7).

Album 1:

Definitely Maybe
Released: 29th August 1994; UK Chart Position: 1; Label: Creation
Track Listing: Rock 'n' Roll Star; Shakermaker; Live Forever; Up in the Sky; Columbia; Sad Song – vinyl only; Supersonic; Bring it on Down; Cigarettes and Alcohol; Digsy's Dinner; Slide Away; Married with Children
Producers: Dave Batchelor, Mark Coyle, Owen Morris, Noel Gallagher

---

Definitely Maybe had something of a chequered history on its journey to the record store shelves, but when it finally made it on 29th August 1994, it became the fastest selling British debut album of all time, shifting 86,000 units in its first week alone.

Going straight in a number 1, the album's initial chart run lasted 131 weeks until 8th March 1997. On and off, it has been in the top 100 ever since. At the time of writing it is at number 54, having enjoyed another run since 21st November 2019, for no reason other than new audiences continue to discover it twenty-five years after its original release. To date it is estimated to have sold 15 million copies worldwide.[xii]

Recording began in December 1993 at Monnow Valley Studio, near Monmouth, Wales, with Dave Batchelor in the producer's chair. Batchelor, who Noel met during his time with the Inspiral Carpets, was probably best known for producing glam-rock band The Sensational Alex Harvey Band, who took a cover of Tom Jones' Delilah to number 7 in 1975.

The studio was so secluded that it could only be accessed via a boat across a river, and with no distractions the band knuckled down and recorded all the tracks in two weeks, at a cost of £800 per day. Unfortunately, the results were not what they had expected. As Bonehead put it, "That doesn't sound like it sounded in that room. What's that? It was thin. Weak. Too clean."[xiii]

The band returned to London with only Slide Away of an acceptable quality, with Alan McGee confirming that the Real People demo Noel had handed him in Glasgow was better quality. Everyone agreed that the issue was that the band and Batchelor didn't gel, and in an effort to capture the sound the band created live, live engineer Coyle, so far only tested in a studio with Supersonic, was drafted in for the band's second, and last, go at recording the album. Had Oasis been signed to Factory, or any other indie label, they probably would not have been afforded a second go, and we might never have had *Definitely Maybe*.

This time the band decamped to Sawmills Studio in Cornwall, where The Stone Roses had recorded their indie-dance classic Fools Gold in 1991. In an attempt to capture the band's live sound, Coyle put Oasis together in one room, so there was no separation between the instruments, and they were able to draw on each other's energy like they did on stage. When the basic tracks were down, Noel layered guitar line after guitar line in an effort to build the dynamics he thought were still missing.

Another two weeks passed and the tracks were still not up to scratch. Now it was time to worry. Out of desperation, Marcus Russell turned to Johnny Marr, who introduced him to the young engineer Owen Morris. Marr, who had produced his own work ever since the first Smiths' recording back in 1983 (when he was just 20 years old), had employed Morris as engineer for the first Electronic album, the band that Marr formed with Bernard Sumner from New Order in 1989. Morris knew his stuff, and with Russell giving him free rein to do whatever he wanted, he set about remixing the second set of tracks.

As well as layering a quarter beat delay to the snare drum to add space to its sound, and taking the top end off the bass guitar (both tricks learnt from Sumner), Morris's key addition was to add an effect to the guitars that made them twice as loud. His little box of tricks saved the day. He stripped Noel's layers of guitars out and kept the recordings raw, giving the band the urgent, energetic, back-to-basics rock 'n' roll record that they had been after.

It perfectly iterated the band's message and connected with its audience in a way that no debut album had since *Please Please Me* back in 1963.

Not surprisingly, Oasis employed Morris to produce their next two albums.

Definitely Now

Definitely Maybe is an album about wanting to be free from the shackles of confinement, while also garnering its strength from those very shackles. It is at its best when the band creatively draw on the things they dream of escaping from. Namely, Manchester, the city that was both their prison and their whole world. Much of the music that shaped them was inspired by their hometown, so, they never managed to fully escape.

Album opener Rock 'n' Roll Star, for example, is equally shaped by the gritty realism of a Smiths' song and the dreamy symbolism of a Stone Roses' track, taking these two key influences and creating something more than the sum of its parts. On The Smiths' 1984 single William it was Really Nothing, Morrissey sings:

> *The rain falls hard on a humdrum town,*
> *This town that drags you down*

Noel borrowed this feeling, shifting it to a first-person narrative for the opening lines to the album:

> *I live my life in the city,*
> *There's no easy way out,*
> *The day's movin' just too fast for me*

On the opening track to the Stone Roses eponymous debut, Ian Brown sings, "I wanna be adored, you adore me." Which Noel changes to: "Tonight, I'm a rock and roll star." The two things were interchangeable for him. He turned the abstract thought into a reality, creating his own relatable kitchen-sink drama in the same vein as Alan Sillitoe's 1951 novel *Saturday Night and Sunday Morning* about a young working-class man rebelling against the system he believes is trying to control him.

People related to *Definitely Maybe* because they shared the band's desire to escape by becoming rock 'n' roll stars. The album draws its strength time and again from its surroundings, losing itself in its dreams, but remaining grounded throughout. For every Live Forever, a song with a distinct ethereal feeling, there is a Supersonic, which hammers home its message: "I'm feeling supersonic, give me gin and tonic."

The album cover, shot by rock photographer Michael Spencer Jones, finds the five members of the band in the front room of Bonehead's mother's house. They are sitting idly around with goblets of red wine and Benson & Hedges cigarettes. Noel sits playing a guitar, Liam lies dreaming on the floor, Tony McCarroll is cross-legged watching the TV. They are a group of teenage boys dreaming of growing up and leaving this room behind by doing the very thing that they are posing for. It was the same dream they had ten years earlier, and which hundreds of teenagers around the country were dreaming themselves when the album was released. The cover's message was not abstract. There were no sliced lemons, Jackson Pollack style prints or semi-naked torsos, the image may as well have had a kitchen sink in the corner.

Oasis were not doing anything new – the accusation regularly levelled that the band's music is derivative is not unfounded – but *Definitely Maybe* is such an accomplished record precisely because it is defined by its influences. Noel took the best bits of his favourite bands and created something of its time with universal appeal. The honky-tonk piano in Digsy's Dinner could be from an Inspiral Carpets song, the echo-drenched guitar solo in Slide Away could have been played by John Squire on an early Stone Roses record, while Bring it Down fits in perfectly with the Buzzcocks punk canon.

But *Definitely Maybe* is not a record that just passively captures a moment in Manchester music history, it is also an act of rebellion. It's a two-fingered salute to the establishment of the late eighties that kept the working-classes from developing artistically. And this is where Oasis begin to come into their own, stepping out from the shadow of Manchester and taking on the establishment, a move that could so easily have blown up in their faces.

"You're the outcast, you're the underclass," sings Liam in Bring it on Down, as much at himself as his audience. And the key message of Cigarettes and Alcohol is how, "You've gotta make it happen." Because no one else is going to do it for you.

As music writer Alex Niven has it:

> *Genuinely progressive upheavals in pop, such as those on the 1960s, have usually occurred at times of relative working-class enfranchisement … If financial and educational resources are withdrawn from working-class communities, as they were emphatically during the period ushered in by Thatcher in Britain and Ronald Reagan in America, one consequence is that musicians turn inwards and backwards.*[xiv]

Noel acknowledged the government's role in keeping the working-classes from developing in Up in the Sky, writing in response:

> *Hey you, up in the sky*
> *Learnin' to fly*
> *Tell me, how high*
> *Do you think you'd go*
> *Before you start falling?*

Although released in August 1994, four weeks after Tony Blair became leader of the Labour Party, these lyrics were written in 1991 as John Major's government was about to push the country into another recession, showing Noel's shrewd foresight and giving them a renewed pertinence.

As much as *Definitely Maybe* trades on its influences, borrowing the riff to Cigarettes and Alcohol from T-Rex's Get it On for example (a standard rock 'n' roll riff Marc Bolan borrowed from Chuck Berry), the record is also a prime example of what can be achieved by the working-class in tough times. This type of single-minded determination formed the cornerstone of Blair's drive to help Britain help itself, but was formed in the heart of Thatcherism, which, in its way, helped to create Oasis as much as they helped to create themselves.

Unlike The Beatles, who already had a number 1 single by the time their debut album was released, or indeed the Arctic Monkeys, who had two number 1s by the time their first album became the fasting selling debut in 2006, the release of *Definitely Maybe* came off the back of three singles that performed well, but not staggeringly so. This meant that its enormous success came somewhat from left field. Everyone was astonished when it sold 100,000 copies and went straight to the top spot in its first week. Everyone, that is, apart from the band's hardcore fans. The album's success made the rest of the county sit up and pay attention. People had heard of Blur by this point, but for new indie music, that was about it. Oasis were about to change that.

UK Official Albums Chart – Top 10 – 4th September 1994:

1. ***Definitely Maybe* – Oasis**
2. *The 3 Tenors in Concert 1994* – Carreras/ Domingo/ Pavarotti
3. *End of Part 1 – Their Greatest Hits* – Wet Wet Wet

4. *Twelve Deadly Cyns… And Then Some* – Cyndi Lauper
5. *Parklife* – Blur
6. *The Holy Bible* – Manic Street Preachers
7. *The Essential Collection* – Elvis Presley
8. *Always and Forever* – Eternal
9. *Brother Sister* – Brand New Heavies
10. *Secret World Live* – Peter Gabriel

You only need to look at the top 10 albums the week *Definitely Maybe* first charted to see how disjointed chart music was in 1994. Three indie-rock bands, three artists trading on former glories, two greatest hits and a live album, but precious little new, interesting music.

Single 4:

Cigarettes and Alcohol
Released: 10th October 1994; UK Chart Position: 7;
Label: Creation; Album: *Definitely Maybe*
B-sides: I Am the Walrus (live – Glasgow Cathouse, June 1994) [Lennon/McCartney]; Listen Up; Fade Away
Producers: Mark Coyle, Owen Morris

After briefly stopping to support the release of *Definitely Maybe*, the Oasis machine took to the road once more, visiting Sweden, Ireland, Germany, the Netherlands, Japan and, by the end of September, the Holy Grail for all bands, America. They then found themselves in France, Sweden, Germany and Belgium before finally returning to the UK for another lengthy tour that ended just after Christmas 1994. In this time, they also released two more singles, Cigarettes and Alcohol and the non-album track Whatever. Both went top 10.

When Cigarettes and Alcohol was released on 10th October 1994, there was almost no band left to promote it, Noel having left the tour after a disastrous gig at the Whisky a Go Go in Los Angeles.

In a pre-social media world, the audience back in the UK had no idea what was going on across the pond and Cigarettes and Alcohol, the band's most in-your-face slice of rock 'n' roll jumped straight into the charts at number 7. After an initial eight week run, it went on to spend a total of 79 weeks in the chart over the next four years, the band's longest to date, again experiencing a bump when the singles collections were released at the end of 1995.

The first B-side is the band's guitar-heavy cover of The Beatles' 1967 nonsensical classic I Am The Walrus, which had been a staple of their live set since their early days and had drawn much attention from audiences who were otherwise often apathetic. Doing nothing to detract from the accusations that they simply mined The Beatles back catalogue for ideas, the cover is at least done in their own style (the original doesn't have any guitar parts on it), and appears here as a live version recorded at the sound-check at Glasgow Cathouse in June 1994, with the audience cheers later added by Owen Morris.

Listen Up, a track that Noel played live at the Royal Albert Hall acoustic concert in 2009, is something of hybrid song for Oasis, seemingly consisting of the intro drum beat to Live Forever and the guitar opening from Supersonic. Lyrically, the song is a considered assault on the ruling classes' penchant for controlling the thoughts and actions of the working class, and how rock music can give the working man a voice and, as a result, his freedom.

> *Listen up what's the time said today*
> *I'm gonna speak my mind*

Take me up to the top of the world
I want to see my crime

Day by day there's a man in a suit
Who's gonna make you pay
For the thoughts that you think
And the words they won't let you say

UK Official Singles Chart – Top 10 – 16th October 1994:

1. Sure – Take That
2. Baby Come Back – Pato Banton
3. Saturday Night – Whigfield
4. Always – Bon Jovi
5. Hey Now (Girls Just Want to Have Fun) – Cyndi Lauper
6. Sweetness – Michelle Gayle
7. **Cigarettes and Alcohol – Oasis**
8. Stay (I Missed You) – Lisa Loeb & Nina Stories
9. Welcome to Tomorrow – Snap! ft. Summer
10. She's Got That Vibe – R Kelly

Single 5:

Whatever
Released: 18th Dec 1994; UK Chart Position: 3; Label: Creation; Album: n/a
B-sides: (It's Good) To Be Free; Half the World Away; Slide Away
Producers: Dave Batchelor, Owen Morris, Noel Gallagher

Every band should release a non-album single to bridge the gap between their first two long players so that fans don't forget them as they record their second album.

In this respect, Whatever was the perfect release for Oasis to see out their first amazing year as recording artists.

Recorded in November at the world famous Rockfield Studios in Wales, where they would soon decamp to record *Morning Glory*, Whatever was an old song that Noel kept back, thinking it needed a string quartet to properly fill out the sound. It's an optimistic acoustic-led builder, once again influenced by The Beatles most accessible material, such as All You Need is Love.

> *I'm free to be whatever I*
> *Whatever I choose*
> *And I'll sing the blues if I want*

UK Official Singles Chart – Top 10 – 25th December 1994:

1. Stay Another Day – East 17
2. All I Want for Christmas is You – Mariah Carey
3. **Whatever – Oasis**
4. Love Me for a Reason – Boyzone
5. Cotton Eye Joe – Rednex
6. Think Twice – Celine Dion
7. Crocodile Shoes – Jimmy Nail
8. Them Girls Them Girls – Zig and Zag
9. Power Rangers – Mighty Morphin Power Rangers
10. We Have All the Time in the World – Louis Armstrong

It's easy to see how the care-free positivity of Whatever fit the changing mood of the time, and if it had not been released in Christmas week, it may well have gone to number 1. As it was, it went straight in at number 3, second to East 17 (the band they were goading in that June *NME* interview), who were at number 1 with Stay;

and Mariah Carey, who was at number 2 with All I Want for Christmas.

In the pre-X-Factor/Simon Cowell world, all bets were off come Christmas week and anyone with the right tune could get to number 1. It was a tribute to Oasis and their popularity that they were able to reach such a high position in a week of such strong sales.

The single's second B-side, Half the World Away, went on to become one of Noel's most lauded compositions. Once again featuring Noel on solo vocals, the simple chord sequence and lilting melody were backed by nothing more than his acoustic guitar, a keyboard line and light percussion (Noel banned Tony McCarroll from the studio in case he ruined the song). There is a yearning quality to the track that again anchors it firmly in Noel's desire to escape his roots: "I would like to leave this city, this old town don't smell too pretty."

By the end of 1994, *Definitely Maybe* had sold in the region of 350,000 copies, going platinum. Whatever gave Oasis their fourth appearance on Top of the Pops, the mimed performance coming three days before the release of the single. They were introduced by soon-to-be rival Damon Albarn from Blur.

CHAPTER THREE
"Never Mind the Bollocks, here's the Sex Beatles", *(What's the Story) Morning Glory?* (1995)

No band could have been prepared for what happened to Oasis in 1995. But, true to form, the lads faced the gathering storm of press intrusion and fan adulation with perfect nonchalance. Whatever hung around the top 20 for most of January, dropping out of the top 100 in early March, and their next single wasn't slated for release until April, which gave Noel the chance to actually write it.

But before that, they returned to the US on 22nd January for a mammoth 32 date tour, on which – amazingly – no major dramas occurred. By the end of March they were back in the UK and in the studio recording the new single. Noel says in *Supersonic*, "There's a strange melancholy to Some Might Say, considering I knew it was going to be number 1 before I even sat and wrote it."

The melancholy perhaps comes from the fact that the song finally allowed him to escape his old life, which made him feel trapped but was also the only world he knew. It may seem like artistic arrogance for Noel to say he knew it would be number 1 before he wrote it, but the truth is more banal – their rapidly growing popularity meant the top spot was theirs for the taking, whatever the next single happened to be.

Owen Morris chose Rockfield Studios for the recording of the next album. This was where Queen recorded Bohemian Rhapsody, and where Oasis would go on to record their most famous songs, including Wonderwall, Don't Look Back in Anger, Champagne Supernova and Morning Glory. For the moment though, they had to contend with what was to become their first of eight number 1 singles.

Single 6:

Some Might Say
Released: 24th April 1995; UK Chart Position: 1; Label: Creation; Album: *(What's the Story) Morning Glory?*
B-sides: Talk Tonight; Acquiesce; Headshrinker
Producers: Owen Morris, Noel Gallagher

There was little standing in the band's way when Some Might Say was released on 24th April 1995, and as the hype began to swell, the single surprised no one when it went straight in at number 1, achieving what no other nineties indie band had done before. Up until this point the number 1 slot had been reserved for Wet Wet Wet, Take That (Back for Good was number 1 for four weeks until Some Might Say knocked it off the top spot) and shocking novelty records by the likes of Robson and Jerome and Mr Blobby. Now here was some serious music from some serious Northerners who championed football, drinking and never hid their love of taking drugs and causing mayhem.

A constant thorn in Britpop's side, the Simon Cowell-created duo Robson and Jerome, actors best known at the time for *Soldier, Soldier* (Jerome would also go on to find cult status as Bron in *Game of Thrones*), took Unchained Melody to number 1 for seven weeks, preventing Pulp's Common People from reaching the top spot. In November, their next single I Believe/Up on the Roof stopped Wonderwall from reaching the top spot.

When Oasis reached number 1 with Some Might Say, the charts were no longer the sole realm of music listened to by teenage girls and middle-aged middle-of-the-roaders. Instead, it now embraced music championed by young men and women who worked hard, drank harder, went to clubs, gigs and football, and who would ultimately come to define youth culture in the nineties.

Guitar-based indie-rock music, and its flag-waving subsidiary Britpop, had now arrived in the mainstream proper and Oasis had achieved what The Stone Roses, Happy Mondays, Primal Scream, Suede, Pulp and even Blur had failed to yet do, pushing them up onto the same platform as their heroes The Jam, The Kinks, The Rolling Stones, and The Sex Pistols (although technically The Sex Pistols' June 1977 single God Save the Queen was never number 1 as the charts had no official number 1 that week). In other words, Oasis were beginning to do for the nineties what The Beatles did for the sixties.

Some Might Say was the perfect song for the time. It is still the Oasis song that sounds best on the radio, its guitar hook similar to T-Rex (and Cigarettes and Alcohol) but distinct enough to be immediately recognisable as Oasis, and its lyrics, while still predominantly nonsensical, somehow manage to capture a British realism snapshot of ordinary life: "The sink is full of fishes, she's got dirty dishes on the brain." Noel even turned his hand to poetic poignancy with the line, "Some might say, they don't believe in heaven, go and tell it to the man who lives in hell."

Track 2 on the single was Talk Tonight, a dark, moody ballad to lost souls featuring a solo turn by Noel on vocals and guitar. He wrote the track about the few days when he abandoned the American tour in October 1994. Not knowing whether he was leaving the band or not, he went to stay with a young American woman who took him under her wing. The song captures his feeling of loss as he stood between two worlds. It would go on to be a fan favourite, being played with the full band in 2000.

Acquiesce was every bit as strong as the A-side (which many thought it should have been). With its guttural guitar riff and anthemic chorus, "Because we neeeeeed each other", the band used it as their opening song (after the instrumental Swamp Song) in live sets throughout much of the following year.

UK Official Singles Chart – Top 10 – 5th May 1995:

1. **Some Might Say – Oasis**
2. Back for Good – Take That
3. Key to my Life – Boyzone
4. Two Can Play at that Game – Bobby Brown
5. Don't Stop (Wiggle Wiggle) – Outhere Brothers
6. Chains – Tina Arena
7. The Changingman – Paul Weller
8. If You Only Let Me In – MN8
9. Have You Ever Really Loved a Woman – Bryan Adams
10. Army of Me – Bjork

The week that Some Might Say reached number 1, pop music continued to dominate the charts, with three boybands, plus the light rock of Bryan Adams. However, with Oasis at number 1 and the modfather himself, Paul Weller, proving he really is a Changingman at number 7, the doors were now open to the developing Britpop scene.

In addition, The Stone Roses were at 29 with the remix of Fools Gold; Portishead were at 31 with Sour Times; and somehow The Beatles were at number 73 with Baby It's You (who knew!). Oasis were also at numbers 88, 90, 91 and 97 (only Whatever wasn't in the top 100).

At the party to celebrate their number 1 single, Liam goaded Blur's guitarist Graham Coxon, boasting how his band were now more successful. Their rivalry had officially begun.

The other significant thing that happened while Some Might Say was at number 1 was that Tony McCarroll was handed his P45 when he was unceremoniously sacked as Oasis' drummer. Tony, a founder member of the group, had been the weakest link from day one, singled out by the other lads as their punch-bag like kids in the playground. Only Bonehead remembers Tony with anything verging on affection, calling him a "soft soul, very Irish in his ways."

Tony's drumming ability was limited, but think of the opening bars of Live Forever; what he played fit the music in the same way as Bonehead and Guigsy. Simple, but perfect for the song. Knowing that there were more complicated songs on the way, Noel finally had Marcus Russell put in the call to tell him his time in Britain's biggest group had come to an impromptu end.

With the indie music world becoming more and more of a closed family, Tony's replacement was Alan White, the 23-year-old younger brother of Steve White, the drummer in Paul Weller's band. Noel saw him play in the studio on Friday, met up with him again the following Monday and, by Wednesday, he was playing with them on *Top of the Pops*. White was a more accomplished drummer than McCarroll and, even though he was from London, he was in. Over time, he became particularly close to Liam, the only member of the group able to keep up with his drinking. White's first gig with his new band was on 5th May 1995 in Leicester. Later that month, they went into the studio to record their second album.

> **Single 7:**
>
> Roll With It
> Released: 14th August 1995; UK Chart Position: 2;
> Label: Creation; Album: *(What's the Story) Morning Glory?*
> B-sides: It's Better People; Rockin' Chair; Live Forever
> (live – Glastonbury 1995)
> Producers: Owen Morris, Noel Gallagher

Battle for the Top Spot

The band headed out on tour around the UK again in
June 1995, headlining Glastonbury on the 23rd – their
biggest and most prestigious gig to date. For many bands
this might have been the zenith of their careers, but for
Oasis, it was just the beginning of a run of record-
breaking gigs. Along with The Cure, their fellow
headliners were supposed to be The Stone Roses, who
had to pull out when John Squire broke his arm – not the
band with the world's best luck – and were replaced by
Pulp.

The rest of the line-up featured the great and
good from the Britpop crowd, including: Elastica, The
Lightning Seeds, The Boo Radleys, Supergrass, Dodgy,
Shed Seven, Reef, The Charlatans, The Verve, and Gene.

Whilst Owen Morris was busy mixing *Morning
Glory*, the band toured the UK and Europe throughout
much of July, during which friction with Britain's other
biggest group, Blur, began to gather momentum.

Ever since Damon Albarn had suggested that
Blur's best album Brit award for *Parklife* should have been
shared with Oasis' *Definitely Maybe* in February 1995,
rivalry slowly grew into mutual antipathy. The two camps
traded friendly blows in the music press but things soon
began to escalate and, much like the rivalry between two

football clubs, their fans chose sides and began to fan the flames.

The story then goes that Damon Albarn moved back the release of Blur's new single Country House, so it coincided with the release of Oasis' new single Roll With It on 14th August. What began as an excuse to engage in some playful banter became bigger than anyone could have predicted. The story even made the news headlines on the BBC, with a spritely Damon Albarn only too happy to play the game, wishing both bands the best of luck, but suggesting that, quite rightly, one of them wouldn't be speaking to the other after it was over.

UK Official Singles Chart – Top 10 – 20th August 1995:

1. Country House – Blur
2. **Roll With It – Oasis**
3. I Luv U Baby – Original
4. Never Forget – Take That
5. Waterfalls – TLC
6. Everybody – Clock
7. Son of a Gun – JX
8. Human Nature – Madonna
9. Kiss from a Rose/I'm Alive – Seal
10. Try Me Out – Corona

With Country House selling 274,000, and Roll With It 216,000[xv], Blur won the battle and Oasis had to contend with a number 2 single. Noel and Liam cheekily swapped places for their performance on *Top of the Pops*, and Alex James from Blur wore an Oasis t-shirt.

Surely it wasn't the end of the world to come second? They had participated in a momentary cultural phenomenon and now everyone could get on with their lives, safe in the knowledge that both acts would sell a shed load more albums through the publicity.

However, this was not the end of it. While Oasis were in Japan in late August news reached them that Blur intended to stage a concert at a venue near their gig at Bournemouth International Arena on 5th October, three days after *Morning Glory* was due for release. "Do you like Blur, I mean as people?" asked Miranda Sawyer, writing an article on Oasis for *The Observer*. "I've got a lot of time for the guitarist. The drummer I've never met him," replied Noel. "I hear he's a nice guy. The bass player and the singer, I hope the pair of them catch AIDS and die … I really hate Damon."xvi

Too far? Undoubtedly, yes, for what had begun as a supposed friendly rivalry. You certainly didn't see John Lennon wishing a painful death on Mick Jagger back in the mid-sixties. The dark side of the football team culture that had bolstered Oasis' popularity now took on the worst facets of terrace rivalry, aspects that saw British football fans vilified all over Europe. Noel was forced to apologise, blaming the time difference during the interview and the pressures of touring. However, Noel knew that Sawyer was going to run the story, and let it be published without making any effort to detract his comment. Noel later issued an apology, via the hand of a press officer at Creation, apologising for using the AIDS reference. Nowhere did he apologise to Damon and Alex.

Roll With It is a catchy enough rock number, and its positioning as the second track on *Morning Glory* and second single from the album fits its second tier status. It's not excellent, it's not terrible, it does the trick and no one complains. The live version of Live Forever (recorded at Glastonbury just weeks earlier) perfectly captures the magic of Oasis at their best. Owen Morris' recorded release of the song was a masterpiece, but there was something in the way Mark Coyle mixed them live that captured the soul of the band.

No one paid much attention to the rest of the singles chart the week that Roll With It reached number

2, but if they had they would have spotted some timeless classics in the top 40, including a number destined to slip effortlessly into the popular music canon to be passed from one generation to the next.

These included: Take That's epic Never Forget; TLC's Waterfalls; Seal's Kiss From a Rose; Supergrass' Alright; You Oughta Know by Alanis Morissette; Ash's Girl From Mars; Edwin Collins' A Girl Like You; a New Order remix, Blue Monday-95; as well as singles from The Charlatans, Paul Weller, The Levellers, Madonna, Bjork, The Pet Shop Boys, Michael and Janet Jackson, Soul II Soul, The Cranberries, Offspring, REM, Black Grape, Pulp, Garbage, Rod Stewart and Annie Lennox.

The jury is still out on whether the Battle of Britpop was a positive thing for the UK music industry, or whether the rivalry fostered an ugly conflict between two acts who should have been championing each other. What cannot be denied, however, is that the music being released in August 1995 in both the UK and America was some of the best of the decade.

In August 1995, just a year after its release, sales of *Definitely Maybe* passed two million.

The concurrent Blur concert in Bournemouth never happened and, distancing themselves from Oasis and from Britpop, Blur were in America when *Morning Glory* was released. This meant they missed most of what happened next, and soon found themselves toppled from their position as the biggest band in the UK. How fickle music can be.

Album 2:

(What's the Story) Morning Glory?
Released: 2nd October 1995; UK Chart Position: 1;
Label: Creation
Track Listing: Hello; Roll With It; Wonderwall; Don't
Look Back in Anger; Hey Now; (insert – The Swamp
Song); Bonehead's Bank Holiday – vinyl only; Some
Might Say; Cast No Shadow; She's Electric; Morning
Glory; (insert – The Swamp Song); Champagne
Supernova
Producers: Owen Morris, Noel Gallagher

UK Official Albums Chart – Top 10 – 8th October 1995:

1. ***(What's the Story) Morning Glory?* – Oasis**
2. *Design of the Decade 1986/1996* – Janet Jackson
3. *Daydream* – Mariah Carey
4. *Greatest Hits 1985-1995* – Michael Bolton
5. *The Great Escape* – Blur
6. *Stanley Road* – Paul Weller
7. *All You Can Eat* – KD Lang
8. *The X Factor* – Iron Maiden
9. *Picture This* – Wet Wet Wet
10. *D'Eux* – Celine Dion

When *Morning Glory* went straight in at number 1,
the rest of the albums chart was packed with music that
would ultimately stand the test of time, including: Paul
Weller's *Stanley Road*; Garbage's eponymous debut; TLC's
Crazysexycool; Portishead's *Dummy*; Red Hot Chili Peppers'
One Hot Minute; Levellers with the aptly named *Zeitgeist*;
Annie Lennox's *Medusa*; Alanis Morissette's *Jagged Little
Pill*; Black Grape's *It's Great When You're Straight … Yeah!*;
Sonic Youth's *Washing Machine*; Supergrass' *I Should Coco*;
The Charlatans' eponymous album; *Paranoid and Sunburnt*

by Skunk Anansie; *Leftism* by Leftfield; The Foo Fighters' eponymous debut; Chemical Brothers' *Exit Planet Dust*; Radiohead's *The Bends*; and Massive Attack's *Protection*.

Guitar music was not the only genre adding real depth to the British musical landscape at this time, TLC, Mary J Blige and Cypress Hill – though not British themselves – were releasing genre defining R'n'B records, and Puff Daddy's mega hit I'll Be Missing You (written after the death of his close friend Notorious BIG) was just around the corner. Meanwhile, homegrown artists Leftfield, Portishead, The Chemical Brothers, Massive Attack and their former member Tricky were pioneering innovative dance/hip-hop, creating totally new music (just don't call it trip-hop; they don't like that).

What was happening was akin to London in the sixties, Manchester in 1989 or Seattle in 1991; Britain was becoming the central melting pot for multi-genre quality music. Acts were being turned on by each other's music, whichever genre it came from. Back in the sixties, The Beatles were the world's biggest rock band, but that didn't detract from the huge success of Motown Records in Detroit, Frank Sinatra and the Rat Pack in Las Vegas, and Bob Dylan and the folk music scene in New York. Success, it seems, breeds success.

In the nineties, it wasn't long before politicians noticed the thriving music industry and decided to turn it to their own advantage.

Defining a Generation

October 2020 marked the 25th anniversary of the release of Oasis' second album *(What's the Story) Morning Glory?* and it is hard to think of another album in all that time that is more synonymous with modern popular music in the UK. Since 1995, the album has spent a staggering 432 weeks on the UK Official Albums Chart (at the time of writing it is at number 33), ten of them at number one. Of the four singles released, two went to number one and two to number two. And the album is currently the third biggest selling studio album of all time in the UK – having shifted some 4,940,000 copies in the UK alone, going fifteen times platinum and, as of October 2018 – just pipped by The Beatles' *Sgt. Pepper's Lonely Hearts Club Band* and Adele' *21*[xvii]. Worldwide, the album has sold in the region of 22 million copies.

While Oasis' debut *Definitely Maybe* took the band out of Manchester and into the music venues and onto the football terraces of the British Isles, *Morning Glory* took them into the living rooms of the world. In the UK, the album became immediately ubiquitous, with every track superglued to the radio for the second half of the nineties, and something like one in every fifteen households in the country eventually owning a copy. It also made an impact across Europe, particularly in the notoriously hard to infiltrate markets of France and Italy, and most impressively, in America, where British bands since the seventies had tried and failed to make their mark.

All this was achieved despite mostly poor reviews. Paulo Hewitt says in *Getting High*, "John Robinson in the *NME* wrote that the album felt like 'the morning after the night before'," whilst David Stubbs at *Melody Maker* said, "*What's the Story* [sounds] laboured and lazy. On this evidence, Oasis are a limited band ... they sound knackered." The only good reviews came from the *Guardian*, other broadsheets, and the European press, perhaps highlighting how the band had crossed over into the mainstream. Just a year earlier, *The Face* had run the iconic headline, "Never mind the Bollocks, Here's the Sex Beatles"[xviii].

Today, it is difficult to strip an album like this away from the modern cultural landscape it helped to define. Alongside Radiohead's third album *OK Computer*, it is hard to imagine what modern British guitar music would sound like without *Morning Glory*.

So, what made it connect with people so resolutely? How does it differ from *Definitely Maybe*, and how did it manage to strengthen the band's identity and further cement them into the musical landscape, enticing a whole new middle-class audience that the band were apparently fighting against?

Morning Glory is not a perfect record. Noel Gallagher's ideas were pouring out at such a rate that Owen Morris struggled to capture one on tape before moving on to the next. As the album was recorded in just six weeks (with Noel absconding for two of them after an argument with Liam), the band probably did not spend enough time in the studio (something Liam noted at the time). And for the many anthemic highs, there are at least two tracks which could have been swapped out. But, after its release there is no doubt that Oasis became a phenomenon. *(What's the Story) Morning Glory?* manages to perfectly capture a band on the cusp of true greatness. Everyone knew who Oasis were after it was released.

Morning Glory is more honed and mellow than the nihilistic *Definitely Maybe*. Which could explain John Robinson and David Stubbs' negative reaction, and why it was welcomed so warmly onto the turntables of the middle-classes throughout the nineties. The pub rock singalongs were still evident in Roll With It, Don't Look Back in Anger, and She's Electric, but out went the Sex Pistols punk stylings of Bring it on Down in favour of acoustic-led tracks like Wonderwall and the deeply introspective Cast No Shadow, tracks reminiscent of John Lennon's more melodious early solo period.

Switching to acoustic to denote song-writing maturity has become a cliché, even parodied in *The Office* when David Brent tells Gareth to "go and get the guitar" to help defuse an awkward situation at a training day.

The distortion heavy barre chords that build every track on *Definitely Maybe* into a wall of sound are still evident on the grunge-influenced title track Morning Glory (fated to go down well on American rock radio), and album opener Hello is a four-to-the-floor stomper of a song that tricks the listener by beginning with the gentle strum of the chords of Wonderwall before launching into the all-out assault familiar from their debut. But Noel also chooses to build the songs through layers of lead guitar lines, guitar effects such as the e-bow, which draws out each note for as long as it's held in place (most notably on the final refrain of Don't Look Back in Anger), keyboards and even the piano; all notable by their absence on *Definitely Maybe*.

Noel's song writing was assured from day one, but *Morning Glory* marked a positive step forward in the development of both his guitar playing and singing. Where *Definitely Maybe* has precious few backing vocals, *Morning Glory* is awash with Beatles and Kinks style layering, set alongside delicate yet robust harmony lines that lifted the group above the pub-rock status that had threatened to define them in their early days.

Perhaps most importantly, *Morning Glory* is the first time Noel takes a lead vocal, on the timeless classic Don't Look Back in Anger. This strengthened his position at the centre of the group without challenging his brother's domain centre stage. The practical band dynamics did not shift, but Noel's continued development as a singer signalled who was in charge and who was the star, once again highlighting what made this band so fascinating. "Oasis' greatest strength was the relationship between me and Liam," says Noel in *Supersonic*. "It's also what drove the band into the ground in the end."

Thematically, *Morning Glory* eschews the dole queue frustration explored on *Definitely Maybe* and focuses instead on the precarious relationship between success and failure. By the time of writing much of the album Noel might have been a bona fide rock star, but his place was not yet totally secure. He has since said that where *Definitely Maybe* is about wanting to be a rock star, *Morning*

Glory is about being a rock star. Although you could argue that the latter classification is more fittingly attributed to *Be Here Now*, Oasis' mixed bag of a third album, which for all its pomp and vigour was as cocaine-fuelled and histrionic as the band themselves.

Morning Glory mixes fantasy with sensibility, drawing on the dreams of escapism but layering them with the reality of what it takes to fulfil those dreams in a world where the real you is wracked with self-doubt and you fear success as much as failure. For years Wonderwall was considered a love song, but it actually exposes a fear of not being able to perform at the top table, or of getting lost along the way: "All the roads we have to walk are winding, all the lights that light the way are blinding."

Even the title of the record is a question. If *Morning Glory* refers to the band's success (the morning of, or beginning of, their glory), then Gallagher turns it into a question by asking, "What's the story?" As if to say, how did we get here, is it just chance? As such, the album betrays a certain fragility behind the cocksure self-assuredness that the band had become known for.

Like many young men of his generation, Noel was averse to exposing his personal weaknesses to the world, but, unlike most, he had the opportunity of washing his soul through the music he created. Perhaps unwittingly, this allowed his audience to see there was much more to him than just a loud and leary football hooligan.

On *Morning Glory* Gallagher manages to be deeply introspective while discussing the superficial trappings of success. On Cast No Shadow he exposes his fear of not being able to properly articulate what he feels, ultimately meaning he will never be able to truly escape where he is from: "Bound with all the weight of all the words he tried to say, chained to all the places that he never wished to stay." Too self-conscious to give people access to his own mind, he sets the song in the third person and links it to fellow indie-rock star Richard Ashcroft. Tellingly, he was careful to dedicate the song to him rather than directly say it was about him.

Noel's raw emotions bubble to the surface in other tracks too; he just can't seem to help it. He says in Hey Now, "And as I fell from the sky I asked myself why can I never let anyone in?" This statement explores his feeling of fragility as he falls, burdened, unable to stop even if he wants to, while exposing his stark fear of allowing anyone in emotionally.

The record-buying public identified with the album because it chimed thematically with the general mood of Britain in the mid-nineties and harked back to the challenges of leaving childhood and entering adulthood, at the same time the country was trying to find a new sense of identity. By October 1995, it became apparent that the beleaguered Conservative government was on its way out at the next election, but few could have predicted the impact New Labour would have. Partly, by employing the help of Oasis.

While picking up the band's third award of the night at the Brit Awards in February 1996, Noel Gallagher told the crowd that there were only seven people doing anything for the youth of Britain: the members of Oasis, Alan McGee and Tony Blair. This statement appeared to finally move Oasis and their many disciple bands away from the counter-culture – historically, the home of indie music – and into the mainstream. But this is not the full story. The band members came of age in the eighties, towards the end of the Thatcher era, and grew up in a very different world to their seventies predecessors. The collapse of the Soviet Union in 1991 was seen as a triumph for western capitalism – for Thatcherism. While she was pulled from power by the very hands who held her aloft throughout the eighties, she had, in effect, been proved right and her mandate accepted. John Major took control, but Thatcher's presence was still felt.

Many believed Labour would win the 1992 election. When Major and the Tories won by a landslide, it was seen as a victory over the old left, led at the time by Neil Kinnock. For Labour to secure power again they needed to shift to the right. Just as post-war Conservatives recognised that they could not dismantle the welfare state implemented by Labour in 1945, New Labour now saw they could not win with blanket opposition to the free-market libertarianism promoted by Thatcherism.

Tony Blair won a huge victory in May 1997 because he made it socially acceptable to vote for Thatcherite policies by marrying them with those of a traditionally left-wing party. New Labour promised not to reverse privatisation or raise taxes, while still spending on education (education, education). Labour moved away from union control and opted instead for a model based on the US Democratic party, where the party is aligned under one all-powerful leader. Socialism as we knew it was dead, and solidarity was left behind in the closed coal mines.

Oasis were not a political band, but they managed to embody the New Labour spirit more than any other. They were working class and had a chip on their shoulder, yet managed to achieve phenomenal success on their own terms, not giving a damn how many feathers were ruffled along the way.

Just like New Labour, Oasis were an autocracy led by one strong visionary. On *(What's the Story) Morning Glory?*, Noel confidently positioned himself as the spokesman for a generation, not yet distanced by millions in the bank and a list of celebrity friends. He was the perfect mouthpiece for those coming of age in New Labour's Britain. Oasis were always the band of the people, but *Morning Glory* took their popularity to a new level – they were no longer just for the working class; now they were for everyone. It could be argued that no band sums up the nineties spirit better than Oasis, and no record does it better than the multi-faceted *(What's the Story) Morning Glory?*

Single 8:

Wonderwall
Released: 30th October 1995; UK Chart Position: 2;
Label: Creation; Album: *(What's the Story) Morning Glory?*
B-sides: Round Are Way; The Swamp Song; The
Masterplan
Producers: Owen Morris, Noel Gallagher

Which brings us to the band's best known single, Wonderwall, which was released on 30th October 1995. Going four times platinum, it sold more than 1.2 million copies in the UK alone, and charted in more than 20 countries around the world. Today, it is the most streamed song of the twentieth century on Spotify, with 975 million streams and counting. It also has the rather dubious accolade of being the first thing that many aspiring young guitarists learn to play.

The band had hoped that Wonderwall would reach number 1 at the same time as *Morning Glory* was top of the album charts, but they were pipped to the post by our friends Robson and Jerome, whose success echoed that of crooner Englebert Humperdink in March 1967 when his song Please Release Me beat the Beatles' Strawberry Fields Forever/Penny Lane to the top spot.

UK Official Singles Chart – Top 10 – 5th November 1995:

1. I Believe/ Up on the Roof – Robson and Jerome
2. **Wonderwall – Oasis**
3. Gangsta's Paradise – Coolio ft. LV
4. Heaven for Everyone – Queen

5. Thunder – East 17
6. Missing – Everything but the Girl
7. I'd Lie for You (and That's the Truth) – Meatloaf
8. You'll See – Madonna
9. Fairground – Simply Red
10. When Love & Hate Collide – Def Leppard

The week Wonderwall charted, six of the band's previous singles leapt back into the top 100, with Whatever getting as high as 80. Other notable songs in the chart were: Coolio at number 3 with the classic rap tune Gangsta's Paradise; Queen at 4 with Heaven for Everyone (the last material Freddie Mercury recorded before he died in 1991); Everything But the Girl with the re-release of Missing at 6; The Rolling Stones with their cover of the Bob Dylan song Like a Rolling Stone, at number 12; The Stone Roses at 15 with Begging You (their final single until 2018); and Elvis Presley at 21 with The Twelfth of Never.

Like all great songs, there have been many alternate versions of Wonderwall over the years. One of the best was by alt-country singer Ryan Adams, but the most famous came from Mike Flowers Pop, who released a fifties-style novelty version just a month after the original in December 1995 which peaked at number 2, meaning the two versions were competing in the chart at the same time. Some radio DJs joked that Flowers' version was the original, leading to much confusion, notably with Noel's partner at the time Meg Matthews, who thought he had written it for her.

Continuing the band's track record for releasing excellent four track EPs, the B-sides were every bit as strong as the A-side. With its staccato guitars and huge brass section, Round Are Way became an immediate live favourite. The song was an ode to childhood, told from a position of nostalgia rather than a desire to escape (a first from the song writer). The Swamp Song, an instrumental heard in two short sections interspersed between album tracks until now, was performed in its full version, with Alan White's charged drums recorded live at Glastonbury and Paul Weller super-subbing on harmonica.

Track 4 was The Masterplan, an acoustic builder with Noel taking lead vocal, which lays claim to being one of the band's strongest compositions (two on one single, all for just £3.99). The subtle yet emotionally charged epic also gave its name to the band's 1998 B-sides collection, suggesting that despite the band's incredible success, there had been no masterplan behind it all.

On 4th and 5th November 1995 Oasis played to the biggest indoor crowds ever in Europe, with two nights at London's Earls Court. Even though both were immediate hits, *Morning Glory* had only been in the record stores for a little over a month and Wonderwall had only been out for a week, so neither had had time to percolate in the collective consciousness and lift the band's status to legendary yet. It was therefore no small feat that Oasis managed to sell out the shows, playing to 20,000 fans a night, particularly after large sections of the press had written them off after Roll With It only reached number 2. Perhaps it should have been Blur playing Earls Court, but they were in the middle of a huge world tour while Oasis were taking over back home.

It was not completely smooth sailing though, and one member of Oasis very nearly didn't make it to Earls Court at all. Bass player Guigsy decided to take a break as he was suffering from nervous exhaustion, and was replaced by Scott McLeod from Liverpool group the Ya Ya's. McLeod played a few live dates with the band, including in America, and appears in the music video for Wonderwall, but he too decided to ditch the band in the States, claiming he missed his girlfriend. The band played the David Letterman show with Bonehead on bass, and Morning Glory abridged to work without a rhythm guitar.

Guigsy's plight was a familiar story in the mid-nineties, with young men in particular suffering nervous exhaustion as they pushed themselves too hard, didn't look after themselves properly, took too many drugs, drank too much, and bottled up their problems (something that continues to plague young people today). Damon Albarn suffered a similar type of depression, as did Alan McGee, who had a drug-induced breakdown not long after he discovered Oasis.

Guigsy returned in time for the Earls Court shows, with Noel giving him a shout-out on stage, "You seen our new bass player? Guigsy!" The gigs were deemed a success, featuring strongly in the *There and Then* documentary released a year later in November 1996. The band even performed with their support act, The Bootleg Beatles, playing I Am The Walrus as their final song.

In December 1995, the band continued to tour America, and featured for the second time on *Later... with Jools Holland*, playing without Liam, which seemed controversial at the time, but somewhat familiar going forwards. They played their new single Don't Look Back in Anger and their cover of Slade's Cum on Feel the Noize, with Noel taking lead vocal on both. This was the start of a series of incidents in which Liam stormed off stage or failed to turn up for concerts, often frustrated because his voice had failed, but just as often because of his constant partying. This led to Noel taking the lead on more and more songs, which simply fuelled Liam's frustration.

CHAPTER FOUR
The Boys from Burnage Take on the World (Maine Road, Knebworth and *MTV Unplugged*) (1996)

Oasis began recording the most eagerly anticipated album since *Sgt. Pepper* in October 1996, the year in which they also began to stretch their muscles playing live. They played to more than half a million people in the UK alone, as well as joining the exalted few to grace the stage of *MTV Unplugged* – except Liam, who occupied a box at the side of the stage with his future wife Patsy Kensit, claiming he had a sore throat. This didn't stop him heckling Noel though.

The year began in fine fettle with the release in February of their tenth single, and second number 1, Don't Look Back in Anger. The song would go on to achieve legendary status in May 2017 (21 years after its release) when a 400-strong crowd spontaneously began to sing it in St Ann's Square, Central Manchester, where they had gathered to commemorate the 22 lives lost in a terrorist attack at pop singer Ariana Grande's concert two weeks earlier.[xix]

Single 9:

Don't Look Back in Anger
Released: 19th February 1996; UK Chart Position: 1;
Label: Creation; Album: *(What's the Story) Morning Glory?*
B-sides: Step Out; Underneath the Sky; Cum on Feel the Noize (Holder)
Producers: Owen Morris, Noel Gallagher

Who the mysterious Sally is has never been revealed, although Don't Look Back in Anger was later dedicated to the Gallaghers' mother, Peggy, the lyric, "Stand up beside the fireplace, take that look from off your face," a reference to her attempts to get her sons to stand still for a photograph. The song shows a maturity in song writing for Noel, the chord sequence and melody one of his most sophisticated to date. The anthemic chorus also fitted in perfectly with Noel's desire to push the band away from pub rock towards stadium fillers.

The piano intro, a simple C/F chord refrain, was lifted directly from John Lennon's Imagine; a homage, more akin to a sample than an imitation, showing Noel's confidence that his audience would know that was his intention. The band would later sample NWA's single Straight Outta Compton, much slower and looped, on their July 1997 single D'You Know What I Mean, a song that was itself a sample, therefore a sample of a sample.

Again, as music writer Alex Niven has it:

> *Oasis offered a rock equivalent to hip-hop's brazen appropriation of pop-historical source material, a musical cut-and-paste that had deep affinities with sampling culture … If Public Enemy spliced together James Brown, Funkadelic and recordings of Malcom X speeches, Oasis wrote songs that glued together the Sex Pistols, The Rolling Stones, Burt Bacharach, Neil Young, Slade, The Smiths and The Jam.*[xx]

Once again, the B-sides were every bit as strong as the A-side. Step Out, another Noel led vocal, was originally intended for inclusion on *Morning Glory*, until Stevie Wonder's agents allegedly demanded 100% of the royalties due to the song's resemblance to his hit single Uptight (not all artists were on board with sampling, as many hip-hop acts experienced to their cost in the early nineties). Rather than pay out, the band chose to drop it from the album, eventually recrediting it to Gallagher/Wonder/Cosby/Moy.

Underneath the Sky was an introspective musing (and contender for the author's favourite Oasis track) featuring a four-part piano solo; while Slade's Cum on Feel the Noize was the band's first cover since I Am The Walrus, and the song they ended the sets with at the Maine Road concerts in April.

UK Official Singles Chart – Top 10 – 25th February 1996:

1. **Don't Look Back in Anger – Oasis**
2. Children – Robert Miles
3. Anything – 3T
4. Spaceman – Babylon Zoo
5. Perseverance – Terrorvision
6. I Wanna Be a Hippie – Technohead
7. I Got 5 On It – Luniz
8. Lifted – The Lighthouse Family
9. Disco's Revenge – Gusto
10. Falling into You – Celine Dion

The week that Don't Look Back in Anger entered the charts at number 1, Wonderwall was still at number 30, and the band were also at numbers 64, 70, 71, 74, 77 and 79. Plus, they were at number 1 in the albums chart, meaning they had achieved the double they had hoped for before Christmas.

While the singles chart was mostly still filled with disposable pop music, the albums chart included some of the greatest works of the decade, with Alanis Morissette at number 2 with the mega-hit *Jagged Little Pill*; M People, who won the Mercury Music Prize in 1994 and were led by former Haçienda DJ Mike Pickering, at 3 with *Bizarre Fruit* (and 76 with *Northern Soul*); The Bluetones at 4 with

Expecting to Fly; *Different Class* by Pulp at 5; *The Bends* by Radiohead at 6 (and their debut Pablo Honey at 39); Paul Weller at 7 with *Stanley Road*; and Michael Jackson at 10 with *HIStory*.

If the charts were, in effect, voted for by the people, then the annual Brit Awards were at the opposite end of the spectrum, decided by a small pool of industry professionals.

In February 1996, Oasis reigned supreme, winning:

- British Album of the Year – *(What's the Story) Morning Glory?*
- British Video of the Year – Wonderwall
- British Group

Paul Weller picked up best British Male Solo Artist; Supergrass, British Breakthrough Act; Massive Attack, British Dance Act; Brian Eno, British Producer of the Year; Take That, British Single of the Year for Back for Good; and Annie Lennox for British Female Solo Artist.

What is probably most interesting is that Oasis' competition for British album were Blur, Pulp, Radiohead and Paul Weller all five guitar-based indie-rock acts, who featured prominently in the top 100 albums of all time lists over the years. The 2006 *NME* list had Pulp's *Different Class* at number 7, Radiohead's *The Bends* at 11, Oasis at 3 with *Definitely Maybe* and 92 with *Morning Glory*, and Blur at 6 with *Modern Life is Rubbish* and 89 with *Parklife* (*The Great Escape* didn't feature).[xxi]

The Brit Awards were held on the same day that Don't Look Back in Anger was released, then broadcast on Thursday 22nd February. Oasis were everywhere. They were top of the singles chart, top of the albums chart, splashed all over the music press and making waves in the mainstream press as the biggest winners at the Brits. This was surely the moment they became the country's biggest band. What was next? The world. They left for another tour of America on 23rd February, returning for UK and European dates on 18th March.

On 23rd and 24th March, they played the 13,000 capacity Point Theatre in Dublin to what felt like a homecoming crowd. The Gallaghers had a clear affiliation with Ireland that dated back to the brothers being dragged – by the ear holes – across the Irish Sea to spend the summer holiday with Peggy's family. As their success grew, so did their familial homeland's feeling of ownership, culminating in the March 1996 shows. Despite their rapturous reception, these concerts turned out to be just the dress rehearsal for two even bigger shows later that year in Páirc Uí Chaoimh in Cork, where more than 100,000 people turned up to hear them play.

Sadly, the Point gigs ended on a sombre note when the brothers bumped into their estranged father Tommy at the bar after the concert. Liam wanted to know how he could even consider selling his story to the newspapers, but Noel managed to keep him away. Tommy had told the *News of the World* that Peggy and her three sons had abandoned him and, spurred on by the red top, Tommy had called Liam, who threatened to break his legs if he saw him. The tabloid set up a hotline for fans to call in and listen to the conveniently recorded conversation. Noel, showing his mettle when it mattered the most, managed to calm Liam down, much to the disappointment of the *News of the World*, and the family reunion didn't happen.

The band returned to the USA for another handful of dates in April on the epic *(What's the Story) Morning Glory?* Tour. They then came back to the UK for their biggest solo headline gigs to date, two nights at "the home of footballing excellence" to quote Guigsy, Manchester

City's ground, Maine Road. The band had not performed in Manchester since November 1995, so these were homecoming concerts for the conquering heroes. Again, the gigs were record-breaking, with the band shifting all 40,000 tickets for the first night in under an hour. When the second night was added, the 40,000 tickets sold out again. The Maine Road gigs went on to make up half the material on the *There and Then* documentary.

Noel famously played his Epiphone Sheraton guitar emblazoned with the Union Jack, which became a symbol for the short-lived Cool Britannia movement that lasted from 1995 to 1997 (Geri 'Ginger Spice' Halliwell wore her famous Union Jack dress at the Brit Awards in 1997). Then in June 1998, the *NME* staged a photo of a similar guitar in flames to mark their "Why British music is going up in smoke" edition.

The band took some time off from May to July 1996, which in Noel's case meant writing new material. On 3rd May, a television programme was broadcast in the North-West, *From the Beatles to Oasis: Forty Years of Granada Pop*, hosted by Tony Wilson, who had returned to his old job of news reporter at Granada after Factory Records closed in 1993, now, presumably kicking himself for not signing Oasis when he had the chance.

On 13th May, Champagne Supernova was released in the USA as a radio single and went straight to number 1 in the Modern Rock Tracks Chart, going gold in the process. Wonderwall too had reached the top spot in the same chart (and number 8 in the Billboard Top 100), but this was the first time they had reached number 1 with a single that was not released anywhere else in the world. Champagne Supernova also reached the top 20 of the Billboard Airplay chart, and even made it to 100 in the UK charts on airplay alone. As 1996 drove on, there really was no escaping Oasis, the hype continuing to build as everyone eagerly awaited their next move.

True to form, their next move would be their biggest yet: a string of enormous live dates across the UK, centred on two concerts at Knebworth Park on 10th and 11th of August. The on-sale date was 11th May at 9am, and approximately 2.5million people applied for tickets. A quarter of a million actually got a ticket. These concerts would historically prove to be the zenith of the band's career, and remain the biggest paying concerts ever in the UK.

Keen music fans will know that Robbie Williams played to 375,000 fans over three nights at Knebworth in August 2003. But as sources claim that Oasis played to 135,000 and 145,000 over two nights[xxii], each of their gigs was bigger. Plus, fewer people applied for tickets to Robbie's show, and, as a tribute to his heroes, he played a version of Wonderwall as part of his set.

Before Knebworth, Noel and partner Meg Matthews (the couple married a year later) went to the Caribbean Island of Mustique to stay at Mick Jagger's place with their friends Johnny Depp and his partner Kate Moss. Noel was incredibly anti-social and forced himself into an eight-hour day of writing and then later recording, soon calling for the support of Owen Morris, who flew out with his eight track to record demos for what would become *Be Here Now*.

These recordings became known as the Mustique demos and were only released in October 2016 (20 years after they were recorded), as part of the remastered release of *Be Here Now*.

The *Be Here Now* demos comprised of 14 tracks, including D'You Know What I Mean, My Big Mouth, Don't Go Away, Stay Young and Trip Inside (later renamed Be Here Now). Having previously demoed just on his acoustic guitar, this was the first time Noel had recorded such professional demoes. Owen Morris was so taken with the result that he wanted to use many of them on the album proper, but he couldn't strip off the drum machine and replace it with live drums, so the tracks all needed to be re-recorded.

The lack of Liam's vocals aside, the recordings show how sophisticated Noel's demo recordings were becoming and, more importantly, his complete dominance over the band's music. By the time they came to record the next album, the other members' contribution was nominal at best, and for Bonehead and Guigsy, the remaining founder members of the group that began as The Rain, their days in Oasis were numbered.

August was a busy month for Oasis. On 3rd and 4th, they played to 80,000 people at Loch Lomond in Scotland; on 10th and 11th, to 250,000 at Knebworth Park in Hertfordshire; on 14th and 15th, to 100,000 people in Páirc Uí Chaoimh, Cork, Ireland; and on 23rd they appeared on *MTV Unplugged* at the Royal Festival Hall.

The MTV gig – the band's last UK fixture until 13th September 1997 – was for just 400 lucky punters, and was a noted success. Unlike the band's usual live set-up, where Liam drew the audience's eyes from centre stage as the huge wall-of-sound surrounded him, with Noel fronting, the band was more suited to the acoustic set-up. Liam's loud, Johnny Rotten voice was replaced by Noel's more subtle, malleable voice that suited his introspective ballads and acoustic versions of the rabble-rousers.

On 25th August, the band were on a plane to the USA, minus Liam, who claimed he needed to buy a house (he had been officially still resident at his mum's throughout all of this craziness), leaving Noel to take vocals at Allstate Arena in Illinois on 27th August. Liam re-joined the band on the 30th at the Palace of Auburn Hills, Missouri, and then stormed off stage at the MTV Music Awards during Champagne Supernova on 4th September.

The tour finished on 10th September and Noel flew home alone the next day to an onslaught of press attention at Heathrow, his solo flight fuelling speculation that the band were finished. They weren't and recording for *Be Here Now* began at Abbey Road Studios on 7th October.

To End all Concerts

In his 2016 documentary *Supersonic*, director Mat Whitecross positions Oasis' performances at Knebworth Park as the climax of the band's success. The concerts bookend his film, which focuses solely on their first five years, ignoring their further five studio albums released before they split in 2009.

In the film, Noel implies that the band should have called it a day after Knebworth ("We should have disappeared into a puff of smoke") while Liam conversely thinks that after finding out how many people applied for tickets, they should still be playing there twenty years on.

Noel says at the end of the film:

> *People make the mistake of thinking that the people on the stage here are defining something. What if no one turns up? We can sit here and suck each other's ball bags about 2.6 million people applying for tickets, but you know what's great about that? It's the 2.6 million people. Not anything that we did.*[xxiii]

As musicians, Oasis were good, but not great. As a band, they were unbeatable, having an undeniable effect on the millions that made up their audience. A huge part of their success was down to timing; they were the perfect band for the time, and Knebworth was the moment that perfectly distilled what they meant to their audience. Noel's songs chimed with the conjoined public consciousness, illuminating what it meant to simply be alive at that moment.

"This is history," Noel Gallagher called to the crowd, sensing the importance of the moment. And it wasn't just because of the record-breaking audience, it was the staggering achievement of a backstreet Mancunian band reaching this colossal space. The Knebworth concerts could only have happened the way they happened in 1996, when creativity, artistic freedom, media exposure and technological advancement gloriously collided.

The Beatles were forced to give up playing live in 1966 predominantly because the technology had not been invented to support the size of gigs that they needed. At the 56,000-capacity Shea Stadium concert in 1965, George Harrison was gifted a 100-watt amp by VOX, made specially for the occasion, but it was played through the baseball ground's normal PA system, which could not compete with the cheering crowd. These days, bands at the 200-capacity Dublin Castle use a 100-watt amp.

The size and shape of the baseball ground also meant The Beatles were separated from the audience by a huge gap, a strange no-man's land between the fans and the band that took up most of the pitch. They had to take a taxi to get to the stage! By today's standards it looks bizarre.

Four years later in 1969, The Rolling Stones performed to an estimated 500,000 people in Hyde Park (the concert was free so the numbers are not verifiable). The performance was excellent – the footage can be seen on YouTube[xxiv] – but it was a pretty miserable experience, with most of the audience sitting static on the ground, smoking weed, flanked by bored looking police officers. With no screens or a big enough PA system, no one had a clue what was going on. Half the audience might as well have not been there.

Then, tragedy struck at the Altamont Free Concert in California in December 1969, when eighteen-year-old African American Meredith Hunter was hounded from the stage and killed by members of the Hells Angels, who the Stones had hired as their security. The mythology around peace, love and freedom that the sixties and seventies portrayed was laid painfully bare. There was no infrastructure to support such large scale concerts, and a life was lost as a terrible result.

At the Isle of Wight Festival in 1970, The Who played to an estimated 700,000 people, who were given a grand hillside view of the stage, but the headliners didn't come on stage until 2am, by which time three quarters of the band (Pete Townsend, John Entwistle and Keith Moon) were so drunk they had no idea what they were doing, while Roger Daltrey was furiously sober. They also had the same issues with sound quality and lack of screens. So, despite its legendary status, it was hardly the best performance from the band or the best experience for the audience.

Elton John and Led Zeppelin developed the stadium rock sound with a string of record-breaking concerts in the seventies, while Live Aid at Wembley Stadium in 1985, and Queen's subsequent concerts at Wembley and Knebworth Park[xxv] in 1986 (Knebworth was Queen's last concert with Freddie Mercury), developed the popularity of large-scale outdoor and stadium one-off spectaculars, which worked in tandem with huge music festivals like Glastonbury and Reading coming to prominence. These events helped to finesse the staging, sound, security, etc, required to make them safe and enjoyable for large audiences. Music festivals have been ubiquitous the world over ever since. The highly successful Lollapalooza four-day festival, for example, began as a touring festival in 1991, and now annually attracts an audience of 400,000.

By the time that Oasis had their moment in 1996, large gatherings of music fans were safe and memorable (in a good way) for both the audience on the day and those watching at home. Advances in recording technology meant they could be released on CD and DVD, just as Robbie Williams did with his Knebworth concerts in 2003. His *Live at Knebworth* album reached number 2 in the UK Official Albums Chart on 11th October 2003 (kept from the top spot by Dido's second album *Life for Rent*). Oasis' Knebworth documentary went unreleased until it was unearthed and loaded onto YouTube in 2017.[xxvi]

After Williams played at Knebworth in 2003, there have been fewer of these massive one-off events. Instead, the focus of live performance has shifted to festivals, where an extensive line-up of acts share the infrastructure, and tours of large-scale venues specially geared up to deal with big shows for big audiences. Coldplay chose to perform to 173,000 fans at three sold out shows at the Emirates Stadium in North London in 2012 rather than to the same number at a one-off concert because the venue was already set up to support such events. Unlike the original Wembley Stadium, which staged outdoor concerts in the eighties, the Emirates had been designed and built with concerts just as much in mind as football matches.

The band doesn't need to provide burger stands, merchandise stalls, ticket collection sites or security offices because the stadium already has them in place. This means they can play to the same number of people and keep costs down. This has become more important than ever since streaming and downloading made music free or incredibly cheap to listen to. In 2020, live gigs are a band's key source of income. They might prefer to play an era-defining one-off concert, but the cost of the hundreds of managers, assistants, production staff, technicians and support staff that are essential to delivering such events to the standard that audiences have come to expect, make it virtually impossible.

Now that most bands rely almost exclusively on their tour earnings and merchandise sales, it's more important than ever they make as much from live concerts as possible. This means that huge Knebworth-style concerts are likely over, which has in turn led to something of a disconnect between act and audience – the exact opposite of what a concert is intended to do. The we-are-one-ness that Oasis championed at Knebworth is much harder to swallow when you have paid £100 for your ticket, £10 for your warm beer and £50 for your tour t-shirt.

Perhaps not surprisingly, ticket prices have risen over the past 15 years to compensate for the loss of earnings through music sales. Some acts see this as fair compensation, while others regard it as an unfair tax on the very people who put the band on a pedestal to start with.

Back in 1996, tickets to Knebworth were £22.50 (around £42.55 today with inflation). The average price for Ed Sheeran tickets in 2019 was £71.40, and he is considered one of the more reasonably priced acts, because he can afford to be, he is one of the few artists in the world who still make plenty from streaming. If an act makes £0.01 per stream on Spotify, then the world's most streamed artist receives £544,421.27 per month income from streaming alone.[xxvii]

The average ticket price for One Direction in 2015 was £130.74, three times the cost of Knebworth, making the gigs unaffordable for lots of fans. For many acts, the price structure can also include five tiers, plus add-ons: VIP passes, golden passes, platinum passes, cringe-making meet and greet passes. Suddenly, the concert tour is a complex, multi-layered beast as intricately constructed as a business enterprise (which is exactly what it is). Add in the cost of travel, parking, snacks, merchandise, and seeing a live gig becomes an expensive business. "How are you all at the back," said Noel at Knebworth. "We can't see you, but we know you're there." Noel cared about his fans enough to make sure they all enjoyed the concert, no matter where they were stood.

The advertised prices for Elton John's O2 Arena concert in November 2021 include £501 for a ticket in the pod closest to the stage, with other VIP packages ranging from £301 to £901. The lowest ticket price is £101 to sit side-on to the stage.[xxviii] This is, of course, an extreme example. Elton charges these prices because his fans will pay them, just as a diamond has no value but that which is placed upon it. You wouldn't catch Harry Styles charging such prices. The VIP experience tickets at his March 2021 tour only cost £165.00. You could see the side of Elton's head for that!

The money-making potential of live music has become most acutely obvious through the plethora of acts that have decided to put aside their differences and play together again. In 1995, The Stone Roses vowed they would never again grace the same stage, but then they reformed in 2012 to play a lucrative tour. The Guns 'n' Roses world tour in 2019 was even called the *Not in This Life Time… Tour*, playing on the band's claims when they originally split that they would never play again in this life time.

Perhaps the biggest difference in music between 1996 and 2020 is availability. Before the internet, popular culture was channelled through the mainstream media, and with only four TV channels in the UK, a handful of radio shows, and no YouTube, you needed to be a popular band like Oasis for the whole country to have heard of you. Music fans all crowded around the TV on Thursday and then Friday nights to watch *Top of the Pops* as their favourite acts – whatever their genre – jostled for position on the country's leading music performance show. Oasis performed on TOTPs three times in 1995, as did Bon Jovi, TLC, M People and MN8. You might not like their music, but you still knew who they were.

In 2020, the Scottish folk/rock singer Gerry Cinnamon managed to sell 50,000 tickets, filling Hampden Park Stadium, without a single article written about him. The Guardian and other mainstream media had wanted to interview him since he started selling out venues in 2016, but he made it clear he wasn't interested in speaking with anyone other than his fans.[xxix] He built a fanbase the traditional way, through touring, but built momentum with an extensive online presence, speaking directly to his fans, keeping control of the message, and deflecting any backlash from unfiltered social media minions as trolling. This is perhaps the ultimate control over your own image, and means that relatively small acts can sell out stadiums without a mainstream media presence. We are drowning in content, but we still need to seek out what's relevant to us. In other words, fans still have to do their bit.

So, Gerry can be content that his concerts are purely for his fans. The audience will have a fabulous time, singing along to every tune, but the event will go largely unnoticed by the wider public. It will not become part of history in the way that Oasis' performance at Knebworth did.

But then maybe that isn't the worst thing in the world, especially if it keeps rock stars more grounded than they have historically been.

Back in August 1996, Noel said that Oasis were: "The biggest band in the world ... bigger than, dare I say it, fucking God."

"When was the last time God played Knebworth?" Liam added.

"He doesn't need to play Knebworth," the Archbishop of Canterbury retorted sometime later. "He created it."

CHAPTER FIVE
Be Here Now: The Rise of Blair and the Decline of Britpop (1997)

Oasis finally managed to free up some space in their collective diary when the recording of *Be Here Now* began on 7th October 1996. Since Alan McGee discovered them in May 1993, the band's schedule had been a flurry of gigs, parties, trips abroad, recording sessions, interviews and TV appearances. But after the end of the colossal *Morning Glory* world tour in America on 10th September 1996, the band could slow down and take their time with their new record.

Where *Definitely Maybe* had (on and off) taken two weeks to record, and *Morning Glory* six, it took the band six months to record *Be Here Now*. This was less to do with perfectionism (although there was an element of that) and more to do with the band's incredible intake of cocaine and Red Stripe.

Liam finally managed to buy a house in Primrose Hill, North London with fiancée, actress Patsy Kensit. The pair eventually married in April 1997, and together made up one of the key power couples of Cool Britannia.

On 9th November, Liam was arrested at the Q Awards for possession of cocaine. He was released later with a caution, but showed no signs of changing his partying ways, despite the band recording the new album. So, with the increased press attention, the band moved to Ridge Farm Studios in Surrey on 11th November to continue the recording, dashing Noel's plans to complete the album at Abbey Road, where The Beatles recorded most of their work.

With the effects of cocaine and alcohol hampering recording, the album took shape very slowly. Owen Morris, who was just as debauched as the rest of them, had major misgivings about the quality of what was being put down. He even tried to use the Mustique demo tapes as the basis for the tracks, feeling that Noel's performances on his own – and without the drugs – were better than what the band were coming up with in the studio. Morris partly blamed the lack of progress on Alan McGee, who he felt should have taken more control, but who in turn passed it back to Morris as the producer, neither party daring to blame Noel or the band.

McGee had only just returned to head up Creation Records, having missed out on much of Oasis' success over the previous two years while recovering from a serious cocaine addiction. You might think that being around a rock group who dabbled on a daily basis might be hard for a recovering addict, but McGee proved his strength early on by spending time, sober, with his other key act Primal Scream, whose legendary drug taking outweighed even Oasis'. But McGee kept away from the studio during the *Be Here Now* sessions, allowing Oasis to record the album as they saw best.

By the end of April 1997, thirty songs had been recorded; eleven picked for the album, the remainder either nominated as B-sides, or in the case of If We Shadows, confined to the shelf until finally seeing the light of day in 2016. So the album was completed, the name chosen, the cover shot, and the video for the first single readied, all in time for Noel to head to the hairdressers and dust off his best suit jacket before popping over to Downing Street (of all places).

On 2nd May 1997, Tony Blair's Labour party won a landslide victory in the UK general election, taking 418 of the 650 parliamentary seats, and so ending eighteen years of Conservative rule. As part of the celebrations, Blair held a party at 10 Downing Street on 9th July for guests from across the entertainment industry. It was a novel gesture; previous prime ministers having only heightened their stuffiness when mixing with entertainers.

His detractors dismissed it as tokenistic, but Britain's youngest prime minister for nearly two hundred years was apparently 'with it' enough to make him feel comfortable with the guests. The opposite of when terminally middle-aged Harold Wilson met the boyish Beatles back in 1964.

Blair's gesture was a thank you to those who had supported his campaign, including Noel Gallagher (remember that comment at the Brits in February 1996), and a showcase for the solid working relationship between New Labour and the entertainment industry. Many felt, however, that this one-off event was a perfunctory brush-off for key industry supporters expecting more than just a party.

Alongside stars of stage and screen like Maureen Lipman, Sir Ian McKellan, Eddie Izzard and Ross Kemp from *EastEnders*, were Alan McGee and Noel Gallagher.

Louise Wener from Britpop band Sleeper says in *Live Forever*[xxx]:

> *It was so depressing when Noel went to Downing Street … He's got his nice neat haircut, and he's got his posh jacket on, and Meg's bought herself a nice new dress, and everything that he was about: that they didn't belong to anybody, and suddenly they did and he was right in their pocket. And in that very instant he was neutered; it was like someone had come along with a knife and cut his bollocks off.*

Noel was not a particularly political person, but he was proudly working class and considered Labour his team, just as he considered Man City his football team. At the party, he took the opportunity to ask the new prime minister what he planned to do for the striking dockers in Liverpool. "We'll look into it," Blair replied with that Cheshire Cat grin, before turning to pose for an awkward photograph with Britain's greatest contemporary songwriter, and then moving on.

Single 10:

D'You Know What I Mean
Released: 7th July 1997; UK Chart Position: 1; Label: Creation; Album: *Be Here Now*
B-sides: Stay Young; Angel Child; Heroes (Bowie)
Producers: Owen Morris, Noel Gallagher

The first new music for eighteen months from Oasis came in the form of D'You Know What I Mean, released two days before the party at Downing Street (undoubtably no small coincidence of timing). Building from airplane noises and Morse code bleeps, Alan White's drums come crashing in, hinting at a military theme that is carried throughout the song. Liam announces rather than asks, "All my people right here right now, d'you know what I mean?"

The song is an epic anthem for the masses, and an astute choice to announce the band's return to the scene. It was the perfect opening track for the new album and became the quickest selling single ever, shifting 160k units in its first day alone.

In what was now classic Noel style, the lyric includes several Beatles' song titles, including "fool on the hill" and "I feel fine". Noel does however make his own mark on the line, "Coming in a mess, going out in style", a reference to the band coming from nothing to reach the heights. This feeds into the overall theme of phenomenal success that filters through *Be Here Now*.

UK Official Singles Chart – Top 10 – 13ᵗʰ July 1997:

1. **D'You Know What I Mean – Oasis**
2. I'll Be Missing You – Puff Daddy & Faith Evans
3. C U When You Get There – Coolio ft. 40 Thevz
4. Freed from Desire – Gala
5. History/Ghosts – Michael Jackson
6. Ecuador – Sash! ft. Rodriguez
7. Piece of My Heart – Shaggy ft. Marsha
8. Free – Ultra Nate
9. Gotham City – R Kelly
10. How Come, How Long – Babyface ft. Stevie Wonder

With at least six urban artists and three dance-pop in the top 10 on 13ᵗʰ July 1997, we can see how hip-hop was developing and dominating the charts. Oasis interrupted I'll be Missing You's three week run at number 1, although it would return to the top spot for another three the following week. Oasis are the only rock act to feature in that week's top 10. The Verve's Bittersweet Symphony at 12 and No Doubt's Just a Girl at 15, the only other rock entries in the top 20.

Although it may seem that Britpop was past its prime, the albums chart showed a shifting away from disposable singles toward long players, with the Prodigy's *Fat of the Land*, Primal Scream's *Vanishing Point*, Radiohead's *OK Computer* and Paul Weller's *Heavy Soul*, all serious, grown-up rock records that would ultimately achieve longevity, occupying the top four slots.

Luckily for fans, who had to cling to the four tracks on the single for a whole six weeks, D'You Know What I Mean was a classic Oasis release on which track 2, Stay Young, was every bit as good as the A-side. Angel Child was another Noel-led acoustic effort in the same vein as Talk Tonight, and Heroes, sticking with the triumphant theme of the single, was Noel's version of the David Bowie classic.

Album 3:

Be Here Now
Released: 21st August 1997; UK Chart Position: 1;
Label: Creation
Track Listing: D'You Know What I Mean; My Big
Mouth; Magic Pie; Stand By Me; I Hope, I Think, I
Know; The Girl in the Dirty Shirt; Fade In-Out; Don't
Go Away; Be Here Now; All Around the World; It's
Gettin' Better (Man!!); All Around the World (Reprise)
Producers: Owen Morris, Noel Gallagher

UK Official Albums Chart – Top 10 – 24th August 1997:

1. ***Be Here Now* – Oasis**
2. *White on Blonde* – Texas
3. *The Fat of the Land* – The Prodigy
4. *OK Computer* – Radiohead
5. *Always on my Mind: Ultimate Love Songs* – Elvis Presley
6. *Backstreet's Back* – Backstreet Boys
7. *Love is Forever* – Billy Ocean
8. *Blurring the Edges* – Meredith Brooks
9. *Spice* – Spice Girls
10. *Sheryl Crow* – Sheryl Crow

With Oasis keeping company with classic albums from Texas, The Prodigy, Radiohead, the Spice Girls and Sheryl Crow, 1997 was shaping up to be a strong year for albums. The emergence of the Spice Girls and the Backstreet Boys from the US showed how boy and girl bands were on the rise again. The Spice Girls debut album went on to sell 10 million copies around the world, while the Backstreet Boys sold a staggering 100 million copies of their six studio albums, making them the biggest selling boyband of all time.

Don't Believe the Hype

Oasis' third album *Be Here Now* was released on 21st August 1997. For thousands of eager fans, it marked the end of a long eighteen-month wait. Taking their lead once again from The Beatles, the title was taken from a quote by George Harrison. When asked what the key message of the sixties was, he said: "Be here, now." The album title helped fuel the press-created image of Cool Britannia, with 1997 marked out as another summer of love, thirty years after the original.

Noel claimed the record was Oasis' *Sgt. Pepper's Lonely Hearts Club Band*. Inevitably, the press were quick to find similarities between the two records. Firstly, they were both predominantly recorded at Abbey Road Studios; they were both recorded over the drawn out period of five or six months; they were released almost exactly thirty years apart; and, unconventionally, both were released on days of the week other than Mondays, *Be Here Now* was released on a Thursday, and *Sgt. Pepper* on a Friday. This gave the record buying public just a couple of days to purchase the records if they were going to push them to the top spot.

Despite the release days, both records went straight in at number 1. *Be Here Now* sold 424,000 copies on its first day, and 695,761 in its first week, making it the fastest selling album in British history[xxxi]. In comparison, *Sgt. Pepper* sold 250,000 copies in its first week of release[xxxii], and went on to become the biggest selling studio album in British history.

But that is where the similarities end. Oasis' record was only their third, while the Beatles' LP was their eighth – and it showed. Where *Sgt. Pepper* is heralded for its innovation in song writing and production styles, *Be Here Now* is criticised as over-produced and derivative, even of the band's own work. With the level of hype built around its release, it was almost inevitable it would fail. Sadly, it earned the somewhat inauspicious title of being one of the most returned albums of all time.

In truth, the album is not as bad as the critics and history have painted it. My Big Mouth and It's Gettin' Better (Man!!), both tracks played at Knebworth, are typical four-to-the-floor stomping rock tracks, perfectly apt for the partying times. Fade In-Out, featuring celebrity mate Johnny Depp on pedal steel slide guitar, is a semi-experimental, semi-country/rock track (bearing many hallmarks made famous by Bon Jovi), and is distinct enough to pique an interest.

The album's best track is probably Don't Go Away, one of Noel's finest fragile ballads writ large with accompaniment from the full band but which would not have sounded out of place played on just an acoustic guitar. The song was later released as a Japanese only import, and remains one of Liam's favourite compositions by his brother. Awash with strings, the track is one of only a few on the album not overloaded with guitar overdubs, opting instead for a subtle tremolo guitar line that accompanies a second verse featuring the poignant lyric, "Damn my education, I can't find the words to say, all the things caught in my mind." This is another momentary glimpse behind Noel's rock star mask at the self-doubt that, in part, dented his bravado.

The remaining tracks fall together as an album should, supporting the feeling in the Oasis camp between 1996 and 1997 that they were now fully fledged rock stars, invincible and impervious to detractors. After the success of the first two albums, and of Knebworth, there was a feeling that whatever happened next was just a bonus. And this is the predominant feeling on the album. The confidence that Noel has in his song writing filters through in the assured melodies. The tracks are all highly listenable as he slips, perhaps unknowingly, from emulating John Lennon's minor key post-Beatles melancholia to Paul McCartney's Wings era major key positivity.

Playing directly into the hands of the gleefully waiting journalists, The Beatles references on the album are more common than they had been before: "Sing a song to me, one from *Let it Be*," sings Liam on the title track; "Fool on the hill" and "I feel fine", from D'You Know What I Mean; and the Noel-sung Magic Pie, which is a partial reference to John Lennon's comment about how he came up with the name The Beatles, when he was "visited by a man on a flaming pie who said you shall be Beatles with an 'a'." *Flaming Pie* was also the name of Paul McCartney's 1997 return-to-form solo album, released a few months before *Be Here Now* in May. Noel was clearly heavily influenced by The Beatles; by 1997 it was what defined him as a song writer, usually bolstering his position rather than detracting from it.

But, with *Be Here Now*, it seemed to have become less acceptable, and the tide began to finally turn against Oasis. Interestingly, their greatest strength – timing – was now the very thing causing their fall.

As the writer Jon Savage says in *Live Forever*, *Be Here Now* "actually isn't the great disaster that everyone says, there are two or three really good songs on it, but it was supposed to be the big, big triumphant record. Labour got in, Oasis are preparing their big statement, and it comes out three or four days before Princess Di gets killed."

It was actually ten days later, on 31st August 1997, that Princess Diana and her partner Dodi Fayed (son of Harrods' owner Mohamed Al-Fayed) were killed in a road traffic accident in Paris while fleeing the paparazzi. And just like that, the public mood changed.

Death in Paradise

Decades are rarely as clearly defined as you might think. The era we know as 'the nineties' didn't start on 1st January 1990. For some, it started, after the end of the '91-'92 recession; for others, in 1989 with the fall of the Berlin Wall (supporting the theory of the long nineties, which includes the years from 1989 to 9/11 in 2001, when on a world stage, the West seemed invincible).

The heady exuberance that came to define the nineties, manifest in *Loaded* magazine, Chris Evans' TV show *TFI Friday* and the music of Oasis, developed in the misguided belief that it wasn't harming anyone. Cheap lager, cheap flights to Ibiza, and relaxed attitudes to sex and drugs all helped to create a semi-disposable hedonistic society. They also had a major hand in building on our existing obsession with celebrity; an obsession that peaked around the turn of the century with *Big Brother*, where ordinary people found fame – and often infamy – simply by being themselves.

Relaxing the strict moral code that had defined British culture since the Victorian age was a double-edged sword. While prime examples of nobility and chivalry were being replaced in the public consciousness by morally questionable footballers and rock stars, popular TV shows like *Queer as Folk* were making gay and queer culture more mainstream, and young women like the Spice Girls were showing that female celebrities were more complex than the traditional angel or whore labels pinned on them for generations.

In music, female artists had generally been viewed through the lens of the male gaze. They were either a Madonna or a Kylie. Madonna's image was purposefully sexualised, with her at the centre surrounded by men, all of whom desire her. She is completely in control, carefully using the image of fifties starlet Marilyn Monroe to position herself as the object of desire. She is one of the two ultimate male fantasies: the whore. Kylie Minogue, on the other hand, took the position of the submissive angel, who, in her eighties heyday was little more than a toy for Pete Waterman to play with.

The Spice Girls changed things up by pushing their 'girl power' message without resorting to taking on traits typical of young men, ie becoming ladettes (although Scary Spice of course did do exactly this). Instead, they were the first girl group seen, not via the men that surrounded them, but through their relationship with each other.

In the pre-smart phone/Instagram/Twitter/TikTok world, the only tool celebrities had at their disposal when it came to creating and controlling their image was the mainstream media, headed up by the most popular and powerful newspapers in the country: the tabloids. This meant that groups of hacks followed the famous wherever they went, even having a key role in driving one of the most famous of all into an early grave.

The death of Princess Diana was Tony Blair's first great challenge, and his handling of the biggest national event of the nineties – including persuading the Royal Family to make a public show of emotion (the subject matter of the Oscar-winning 2007 Stephen Frears' film *The Queen*) made any thoughts of high-tea with celebrities at Downing Street seem trivial in comparison. Paradoxically, it was the power of celebrity and popular music that harnessed the mood of the nation and gave a focus to the immense outpouring of grief.

Elton John and Bernie Taupin originally wrote Candle in the Wind for Marilyn Monroe. But Taupin rewrote the famous "Goodbye Norma Jean" lyric to focus on the life of Princess Diana, changing it to "Goodbye England's Rose". Elton performed it in Westminster Abbey at Diana's funeral and gave the nation a musical peg to hang their grief on.

The single became the Guinness Book of Records' biggest selling single since records began. White Christmas by Bing Crosby has almost certainly sold more copies (it was released in 1954), but records weren't kept back then to prove it. Released on 13th September 1997, the single went straight in at number 1, spending five weeks at the top spot, and preventing Oasis from claiming their third number 1 in a row.

Single 11:

Stand by Me
Released: 22nd September 1997; UK Chart Position: 2;
Label: Creation; Album: *Be Here Now*
B-sides: (I Got) The Fever; My Sister Lover; Going Nowhere
Producers: Owen Morris, Noel Gallagher

UK Official Singles Chart – Top 10 – 28th September 1997:

1. Candle in the Wind ('97)/ Something About the Way You Looked Tonight – Elton John
2. **Stand by Me – Oasis**
3. Sunchyme – Dario G
4. Arms Around the World – Louise
5. Tubthumping – Chumbawamba
6. Got 'til It's Gone – Janet ft. Q-Tip & Joni Mitchell
7. Please – U2
8. Just for You – M People
9. Men in Black – Will Smith
10. The Drugs Don't Work – The Verve

Reaching number 2 was something of a sobering drag back to reality for Oasis, a reminder that there was a world outside of their kingdom. The Spice Girls, Oasis' only real challengers to the UK's biggest act of the nineties, also experienced a reality check when their seventh single, Stop, failed to reach the top spot in March 1998, taking second place to the remix of Run DMC's It's Like That. It was much more painful for the Spice Girls because every one of their previous six singles had reached number 1, making history in the process.

But Oasis were used to reaching number 2, having lost out to Blur in August 1995, emerging not just intact, but stronger than ever.

The B-sides on Stand by Me were equally strong: (I Got) The Fever, a classic riff-led rock belter; My Sister Lover, a reference to The Sister Lovers, the band led by Alan McGee's ex-girlfriend Debbie Reynolds, who offered Oasis part of their slot at King Tuts; and Going Nowhere, an acoustic, brass-led builder that remains one of Noel's most understated gems.

The *Be Here Now* world tour began in the Norwegian capital of Oslo on 8th September 1997, with the band playing their first gig in the UK for more than a year in Exeter on the 13th. After Stand by Me was released, there was a 13-date tour of UK stadiums, including three nights at Earls Court from the 25th to the 27th, supported by their old tour mates The Verve. Back in 1993, when they were starting out, Oasis supported The Verve and were now repaying the favour by giving them three nights as their special guests at one of London's premier venues, just a few days before they released their own comeback record, the era-defining album *Urban Hymns*, on 29th September.

With acoustic-led tracks that could have come directly from Noel Gallagher's guitar, mixed with their standard echo-drenched space-rock, The Verve distilled everything they had into their third album, and the result was one of the last great records of the nineties. With the death of Diana leading the record buying public in a more thoughtful, introspective and much darker direction, *Urban Hymns* sat alongside serious records like Blur's *Blur* album, Radiohead's *OK Computer* and Spiritualized's *Ladies and Gentlemen We are Floating in Space...*, which were all released in 1997.

The popularity of these records, and the subsequent development of more introspective newer acts such as Coldplay, Travis and Snow Patrol, acted as a paradigm shift, moving the zeitgeist away from the pomposity of *Be Here Now* and Britpop. This new direction, in part influenced by the paranoia of Y2K and the impending end of the century, would ultimately shift Oasis away from relevance, and down a parallel path along which they would never properly return.

If Oasis cared about any of this then they certainly didn't show it. With their European and UK dates behind them, they headed out on their most expansive series of dates on 9th January, starting off with a month of stadium performances in the USA. They also released the third and final single from *Be Here Now*, their last single until February 2000, and their last new music of the millennium, All Around the World.

Single 12:

All Around the World
Released: 12th January 1998; UK Chart Position: 1;
Label: Creation; Album: *Be Here Now*
B-sides: The Fame; Flashbax; Street Fighting Man
(Jagger/Richards)
Producers: Owen Morris, Noel Gallagher

Footage featured in *Supersonic* shows the band playing a version of All Around the World in their rehearsal space sometime in 1991. This means that Oasis' last new music of the millennium has direct links with the band's beginning. Noel held the song back until they could afford the full orchestra that helps build the nine-minute epic toward its climactic conclusion.

UK Official Singles Chart – Top 10 – 28ᵗʰ September 1997:

1. **All Around the World – Oasis**
2. Never Ever – All Saints
3. Bamboogie – Bamboo
4. No Surprises – Radiohead
5. My Star – Ian Brown
6. Renegade Master '98 – Wildchild
7. High – Lighthouse Family
8. Together Again – Janet Jackson
9. Angels – Robbie Williams
10. Perfect Day – Various Artists

The song went straight in at number 1, knocking Never Ever by All Saints (whose line-up included Nicole Appleton, later Liam's second wife) from the top spot; ahead of Radiohead's No Surprises at number 4, and the return of King Monkey himself, The Stone Roses' former singer Ian Brown, at 5 with My Star. Other than that, this is largely a top 10 of straightforward pop acts, with All Saints, Janet Jackson, the Lighthouse Family and Mr 2000s himself, Robbie Williams.

Thanks to their box sets, Oasis also had six of their first eight singles in the chart, as well as D'You Know What I Mean and Stand by Me, meaning they had nine singles in the top 100 the week that All Around the World reached number 1. They might not have been as relevant as they once were, but Oasis' popularity was as strong as ever.

Meanwhile, the *Be Here Now* tour continued, taking in Japan, China, Australia, New Zealand,

Argentina, Chile, Brazil, and finally Palacio de los Deportes in Mexico City on 25th March 1998. This was the band's final live performance until 3rd December 1999, and they didn't release any new music until February 2000. By then, the band was a very different beast to the one that played that night in Mexico.

But, back in 1998, Oasis still had something else in store for their fans. Another album was released that year and it was called *The Masterplan.*

CHAPTER SIX
Behind the Band: _The Masterplan_ (a Look at the Band's B-Sides, and Behind the Scenes) (1998)

B-sides Album:

The Masterplan
Released: 2nd November 1998; UK Chart Position: 2;
Label: Creation
Track Listing: Acquiesce; Underneath the Sky; Talk
Tonight; Going Nowhere; Fade Away; The Swamp
Song; I Am the Walrus (live – Glasgow Cathouse, June
1994) [Lennon/McCartney]; Listen Up; Rockin' Chair;
Half the World Away; (It's Good) To be Free; Stay
Young; Headshrinker; The Masterplan
Producers: Dave Batchelor, Mark Coyle, Owen Morris,
Noel Gallagher

UK Official Albums Chart – Top 10 – 8th November 1998:

1. _The Best of 1980-1990 & B-Sides_ – U2
2. **_The Masterplan_ – Oasis**
3. _Supposed Former Infatuation Junkie_ – Alanis Morissette
4. _I've Been Expecting You_ – Robbie Williams
5. _The Best Of_ – M People
6. _Quench_ – The Beautiful South
7. _Hits_ – Phil Collins
8. _Talk on Corners_ – The Corrs
9. _B'Witched_ – B'Witched
10. _The Star and the Wiseman – The Best Of_ – Ladysmith Black Mambazo

Christmas (which for record stores in the nineties began in early November) has always been when record companies release money-spinning "best of" collections. Including U2, who beat Oasis to number 1 that week, there were 12 best of collections in the top 40 when *The Masterplan* first charted. The best ofs and hits collections aside, however, what we see populating the albums chart in early November 1998 is a different musical world from 1997. The likes of Radiohead, The Verve, Massive Attack, and the Prodigy have been replaced by The Beautiful South, Robbie Williams, The Corrs and girl-band B'Witched, all pure pop acts.

As James Oldham said in his *NME* review of *The Masterplan*, "It tells you everything you need to know about 1998 that the release of this album should be cause for celebration. *The Masterplan* might be Oasis' third best album, a compilation destined for foreign fields and a collection of songs that most UK households own at least once already, but it's still Everest to the rest of this year's K2s."xxxiii It was not an auspicious year for new music, with many claiming, like the *NME* had done in their "Why British music is going up in smoke" edition in June 1998, that the death of Britpop meant there was no quality new music.

Luckily that was not entirely true, and 1998 saw the release of the tender but bleak melancholia of the Manic Street Preachers' sixth album *This is My Truth Tell Me Yours*; *Decksandrumsandrockandroll* from hip-hop/dance act the Propellerheads; *Unfinished Monkey Business*, Ian Brown's debut; *Mezzanine* from Massive Attack; *Hello Nasty* from The Beastie Boys; and, of course, *This is Hardcore* from Pulp.

But what about those best ofs? Were the record companies releasing best ofs because there was no new music to release? Or were the best ofs blocking the release of new music?

If we look back at 15th November 1997, the Spice Girls were at number 1 with their second album *Spiceworld*, and The Verve were at number 2 with *Urban Hymns*, but there were also 11 best ofs in the top 40, with four in the top 10: *The Greatest Hits of* Eternal at 3; *Paint the Sky with Stars The Best of* Enya at 4; *Lennon Legend – The Very Best of* John Lennon at 6; and *Queen Rocks* at 7.

On 10th November 1996, the Spice Girls were at number 1 with their first album, *Spice*, and the Beautiful South were at 2 with their huge album *Blue is the Warmest Colour*, and there were eight best ofs in the top 40, with three in the top 10: East 17's *Around the World – The Journey So Far* at 3; Simply Red's *Greatest Hits* at 3; and *Recurring Dream – the Very Best of* Crowded House at 9. So, not a dissimilar situation to 1998. Perhaps nothing changes and record companies will put out quality albums – but they need quality work to release in the first place.

What singled out the Oasis album from all the other collections was that it was comprised purely from B-sides. Even U2, who were probably the only other group that could lay claim to world's biggest band at this point, included their B-sides collection among a host of safe classics.

The Oasis tracks were already so familiar that the casual listener could be forgiven for thinking *The Masterplan* was a best of. The band's cover of The Beatles' I Am The Walrus featured heavily in the live set for the *Morning Glory* tour (and reached right back to their very early days), as did the epic title track, while the opening track Acquiesce, reached number 24 in the US Modern Rock Chart in April 1998 on airplay alone. Half the World Away had been used as the theme tune for the BBC comedy *The Royle Family*, its gentle melancholia fitting in perfectly with this slice-of-life study of a working-class family; and Fade Away was rerecorded for the *Help Warchild Album* in September 1995.

If the album tracks were Liam's familiar ground, the often introspective, acoustic material reserved for the band's B-sides were more Noel's territory, and fans may have expected more from him on lead vocals. But the track listing was actually decided by the people via the band's website (an early example of people power when the internet was still in its infancy). It's a shame that the likes of Take Me Away and D'You Wanna Be a Spaceman, Step Out, or Round Are Way were not included, but the choice of tracks says something about the popularity of Liam as the lead singer.

The album sold 2m copies worldwide. How many other acts can say that about a B-sides collection?

The end of Creation and the beginning of Big Brother

The Masterplan was the band's final release through Creation Records and, as such, a parting of the ways with the man who discovered them, Alan McGee. Since getting himself back on his feet in 1995, McGee had become disillusioned with the label he started in his front room in 1983. He wanted a new start with a new slate of acts. The company went into liquidation in 1999, their final release being Primal Scream's sixth studio album *XTRMNTR* in January 2000.

Oasis had originally signed a six-album deal with Creation and their parent company Sony (releasing records worldwide through their subsidiary Epic), but with the demise of Creation, all bets were off, and the band signed another six-album deal directly with Sony in 1999. The deal was similar to the original, in that Epic took rest of the world rights, and Oasis decided what records were released in the UK and Ireland through their new label Big Brother Recordings. Band manager Marcus Russell was, and is, the managing director of Big Brother, whose debut release was the first new music of the new millennium, February 2000's number 1 single Go Let it Out.

Through Sony BMG (now Sony Music Entertainment), Big Brother and Oasis released: *Standing on the Shoulder of Giants* (2000), *Familiar to Millions* (live album – 2000), *Heathen Chemistry* (2002), *Don't Believe the Truth* (2005), the official soundtrack to the feature film *Goal!* (2005), and their first best of album, *Stop the Clocks* (2006). Noel had made it clear the band would never release a best of while they were still together, but changed his mind in a bid to complete the six album deal with Sony and move onto different working practices. He took over curation of the record to ensure it was made up of songs that he wanted. If it was going to be done, he wanted it done right.

The other business matter that concerned Oasis as they moved into the second phase of their career was the small matter of their back catalogue. Since 1992, Sony had owned 50% of Creation, and so inherited its entire catalogue in 1999 when it folded. One of Big Brother's first actions was to spend 2001 and 2002 buying back the UK and Irish rights to Oasis' early material, subsequently re-releasing the first three albums, the B-sides album, and 12 singles (as well as the *Live by the Sea* VHS/DVD).

Each new release was given the prefix RKID (or 'our kid') and was numbered sequentially, so Go Let it Out is RKID001. So far, the label has had 74 releases, including the Happy Mondays 2005 standalone single Playground Superstar as RKID034, which was taken from the *Goal!* soundtrack and is, to date, the only non-Oasis release from the label.

The film, directed by Danny Cannon, is the rags to riches story of Santiago Muñez, a Mexican illegal immigrant spotted by a former Premiership footballer in America and brought to England for a trial with Newcastle United. The soundtrack featured three Oasis songs, including Cast No Shadow, produced by Unkle with Noel taking the lead, Morning Glory remixed by Dave Sardy, plus the previously unreleased track Who Put the Weight of the World on My Shoulders?. Other bands featured included The Bees, Dirty Vegas, Zero 7, and Oasis' successors Kasabian.

In September 2007, the deal with Sony done, Oasis released the *Lord Don't Slow Me Down* documentary and live gig DVD, and the accompanying single of the same name (which was download only) through a new partnership with Universal Music. This relationship didn't last though; less than a year later in June 2008, a time when big acts were looking for more unconventional ways of creating relationships with record labels, the band signed a first-of-its-kind worldwide three album deal with their old home Sony BMG. In a music industry dominated by streaming, bands now garnered most of their income from gigs and merchandise rather than traditional record sales. Oasis' innovative new deal meant they could release whichever records they wished, with a split profits system in place. Warner Music Group then signed the band to a North American distribution deal in July 2008, which meant Oasis had the full set, working with all the major 'Big Three' labels.

Unfortunately, Oasis didn't reap all the potential benefits of this new style relationship as they split in August 2009, less than a year after the release of their album *Dig Out Your Soul*. Their final release was the greatest hits album *Time Flies … 1994-2009*, in June 2010. To celebrate Oasis' twentieth anniversary, Big Brother Recordings released box set editions of the band's first three albums in 2014, 2015 and 2016.

It's also worth noting that Noel Gallagher quit taking drugs on 5th June 1998. Despite having a strong tolerance, the panic attacks, and the mornings spent wondering who on earth half the people in his house were while chugging on a Red Stripe became too much, so he decided to kick the habit for good. For him, the recording of the band's next album would be a drink and drug-free zone, although the fug of Benson & Hedges would still fill the studio.

Noel had married Meg Mathews in June 1997 and she gave birth to their daughter Anais in January 2000. The couple gave up their Primrose Hill house, the infamous Supernova Heights in Belsize Park, North London, in 1999, and moved to suburban Surrey.

With domestic bliss slowly taking over the life of the once famous party boy, it seemed that change was in the air for the band too. The Oasis the world had come to know in 1994-1998 was soon to be replaced by a new and improved version: Oasis 2.0.

CHAPTER SEVEN
Standing on the Shoulder of Giants and Oasis 2.0 (1999-2000)

The band that reconvened in early 1999 to discuss recording what would become their fourth album, *Standing on the Shoulder of Giants*, was not the same band that had finished the *Be Here Now* tour the previous March.

What had begun as a distraction from the dole queue and the Haçienda, had spiralled to become much bigger than they, or anyone else, could have ever imagined. As 1999 began to slip away, and the end of the century loomed, fate shifted its focus away from Oasis, making the band victims of the very thing that had once made them so vital: timing. With other groups and artists now filling the column inches once dominated by the Gallagher brothers, the feeling began to spread in the band and among the wider public that they were not as relevant as they once were.

The band were no longer a young, vibrant, cutting-edge indie-rock outfit. Instead, they were pampered family men, living in huge mansions, a million miles away from the streets of Burnage. Playing and recording had become a job and, eventually, a chore, particularly as they were expected to be away from home for long periods of time. Noel didn't want to disband the group, and he certainly wasn't ready for a solo career, but he also didn't think he had it in him to write and record a new album either. Of all people, it was the eternal party boy Liam who stepped up to push the band through this difficult period, encouraging his brother to write a new record, and even contributing his first composition.

What Noel discovered as he started to put pen to paper and finger to fret board was that not being as relevant as you once were was, in itself, something to write about.

He duly wrote nine tracks for the new album, and a handful of typically strong B-sides, and recording began at his home studio before quickly moving to Olympic Studios in Barnes and finally to the Château de La Colle Noire, Montauroux, in the South of France, the band deciding to sequester themselves to make sure they got something done.

Shortly after their arrival in the South of France, Bonehead and Guigsy left the group in short succession. This was no real surprise to anyone. The pair had been happy to sit in the background, playing the simple barre chords and root notes that made Oasis songs what they were, but with the heady days of Knebworth and *Be Here Now* behind them, and growing families back in England, they felt they had nothing more to prove, and so quietly slipped away.

Showing that the old abrasive Noel was still there despite the change of mood, he was unable to resist saying that Bonehead leaving the group was "hardly like Paul McCartney leaving The Beatles". Neither of them was replaced until after the album was finished; Noel played both their parts.

The band also decided not to ask Owen Morris to produce the record, choosing to draw a line under the last three albums, which could be considered their Britpop trilogy. Instead, they turned to Mark 'Spike' Stent, whose eclectic back catalogue as producer included: Massive Attack's *Protection* (1994) and *Mezzanine* (1998), Björk's *Homogenic* (1997) and the Spice Girls' *Spice* (1996) and *Spice World* (1997).

Stent was predominantly employed because of his wide-ranging experience at the mixing desk, which meant the band – or, to all intents and purposes, Noel – could be confident he would be able to replicate their vision. Not an easy ask, especially as Noel was still working out exactly what that vision was when they began recording. This was another first for the group, who had always gone into the studio knowing what the album would sound like.

The move was successful, and Stent achieved a level of consistency across the tracks that emphasised the experimental, psychedelic sound of the album. This new sound was mostly created through Noel's array of effects pedals and analogue keyboards, such as the Beatles-favoured mellotron on first single Go Let It Out. The album's tone also hinted at Noel's state of mind; the songs more melancholic than before, with minor seven chords layered with mournful lilting melodies and a message that the Britpop party was a finally over. Just like Pulp's *This is Hardcore* and Blur's *Blur*, *Standing ...* was Oasis' comedown record, the antithesis of the bloated exuberance of *Be Here Now*.

Single 13:

Go Let It Out
Released: 7th February 2000; UK Chart Position: 1;
Label: Big Brother; Album: *Standing on the Shoulder of Giants*
B-sides: Let's all Make Believe; (As Long as They've Got) Cigarettes in Hell
Producers: Mark Stent, Noel Gallagher

Big Brother Recordings' inaugural release was Oasis' first new music of the new millennium, and the first Oasis single to feature just three tracks. New chart rulings, which remain in place today, meant that to be eligible for the UK Official Singles Chart a release was limited to just three tracks. This was partly to differentiate between single, EP and LP releases, but also to give pop acts, who were more limited in their material, the same level playing field as rock and dance acts, some of whom were releasing singles with up to seven or eight remixes of the lead track.

For Oasis, this meant more streamlining of material, with Noel no longer duty bound to write and record new material for the sake of it. With this in mind, Go Let It Out was something of a return to form; the two B-sides equally as good as the A-side. *Q* magazine even included Let's all Make Believe in its top 500 songs of the year. Similarly, the Noel-sung (As Long as They've Got) Cigarettes in Hell sums up his state of mind at the time. The lyrics, set alongside one of his most sombre melodies, find the band's driving force in a decidedly reflective mood, but with his trademark dry wit still intact:

> *I don't mind not feeling immortal,*
> *Because it ain't all that as far as I can tell,*
> *And I don't mind not going to heaven*
> *As long as they've got cigarettes in hell*

The first new material for over a year, Go Let It Out was something of a surprise for Oasis fans. On one hand, it was familiar, with Liam's elongated vowels in fine form; on the other, it sounded like nothing they had done before. After calling for the world to "lock up your sequencers!"[xxxiv] in 1994, here was the world's leading rock 'n' roll band using a hip-hop sampled drum loop to intro their new single. The lyric too proved characteristically difficult to decipher – go let what out? – but the song was suitably listenable and, after a few plays on the radio, it resonated with its audience, reminding them that their favourite band, albeit in a slightly different variation, were back.

With Guigsy gone, Noel took to playing bass with verve and, alongside the band's modern use of a drum loop, Go Let it Out features a prominent bass line; one that Noel deemed important enough to play himself in the music video. This meant that his usual lead guitarist space required a stand-in. Enter Gem Archer, formerly of Heavy Stereo, another Creation band, who Noel asked to join the group in late 1999. Archer's first performance was in the video for Go Let it Out (in which Liam also played guitar, having taken time off to teach himself to play) His positioning made it clear from the off that he wasn't simply taking Bonehead's place, he was also taking some of the band's lead guitar lines too.

UK Official Singles Chart – Top 10 – 13th February 2000:

1. **Go Let it Out – Oasis**
2. Rise – Gabrielle
3. Move your Body – Eiffel 65
4. Adelante – Sash!
5. Dolphins were Monkeys – Ian Brown
6. Born to Make you Happy – Britney Spears
7. The Great Beyond – REM
8. Must be the Music – Joey Negro ft. Taka Boom
9. Glorious – Andreas Johnson
10. A Little Bit of Luck – DJ Luck & MC Neat

Indie-rock and dance-pop acts took something of a backseat as the new millennium got underway, with pure pop acts dominating the singles charts. With no major scene on the horizon, the major labels were beginning to show a lack of imagination, and there was little interesting new music being released. To labour the point, John Lennon's Imagine was hanging around at number 45 the week of 13th February, having been rereleased to mark the new millennium and reaching number 3.

This shows how divisive music had become. On one hand we have the predominantly happy bubble-gum pop, and on the other, the diametrically opposed, negatively charged rock and indie music.

Album 4:

Standing on the Shoulder of Giants
Released: 28th February 2000; UK Chart Position: 1;
Label: Big Brother
Track Listing: Fuckin' in the Bushes; Go Let it Out;
Who Feels Love?; Put Yer Money Where Yet Mouth
Is; Little James (L Gallagher); Gas Panic!; Where Did it
All Go Wrong?; Sunday Morning Call; I Can See a
Liar; Roll it Over
Producers: Mark Stent, Noel Gallagher

UK Official Albums Chart – Top 10 – 5th March 2000:

1. ***Standing on the Shoulder of Giants* – Oasis**
2. *The Man Who* – Travis
3. *Supernatural* – Santana
4. *Rise* – Gabrielle
5. *Come on Over* – Shania Twain
6. *On How Life Is* – Macy Gray
7. *Machina/The Machines of God* – Smashing Pumpkins
8. *Daisies of the Galaxy* – Eels
9. *Play* – Moby
10. *Baby One More Time* – Britney Spears

Unlike the singles chart in early 2000, rock music was still going strong in the albums chart, and one of the key things to note was the return of American music. Britney Spears might have always had an audience, but the death of Britpop heralded a return for rock acts, here represented by the Smashing Pumpkins, Eels and the dance/trip-hop/rock of Moby's mega-hit album, Play.

The Britpop legacy continued in the form of Oasis' one-time support act Travis, and the emergence later that year of Coldplay, but American rock was on its way back to Britain, with nu-metal just around the corner.

Shoulder Standing

By the standards of nearly any other act on the planet, *Standing on the Shoulder of Giants* was a hugely successful album, going twice platinum in the UK (*Be Here Now* went 6x and *Morning Glory* 15x), reaching the top 20 in sixteen countries around the world, and going on to sell 3 million copies. After just one week at the top spot, its initial chart run in the UK lasted for thirty weeks, with thirty-five weeks in the top 100 in total. As we will come to see though, much of this success was due to the lasting loyalty of the band's vast fanbase, rather than the band repositioning its finger on the pulse of the nation.

In some ways, this period and this album are the most important of the band's career. With just three of the band members left throughout its recording, and some of Alan White's parts being replaced by a computer, the band had finally been distilled to its core essence: the relationship between Liam and Noel. The album stands juxtaposed to *Be Here Now*, with the layers of cocaine-fuelled interlocking guitar licks exchanged for simple strummed acoustic chords and haunting mellotrons. Where on their third album the band demanded that we join them in the moment: be here, now; *Standing …* finds Noel asking more questions: Where Did it All Go Wrong? Who Feels Love?; dreaming about being elsewhere: Let's All Make Believe; detailing the paranoiac effect fame has had on his state of mind: I Can See a Liar, Gas Panic!; and even musing on death: Cigarettes in Hell.

Gone is the sense of invincibility, replaced by an introspective yearning for something else, something more solid. It is no coincidence that Noel's first child

Anais was born just before the album came out in January 2000, and Liam's contribution, the first by any songwriter other than Noel, isn't about partying or escaping the confines of the city you grew up in, but is another ode to domesticity. In this instance, Little James was written for Liam's stepson, James, the son of Patsy Kensit and Jim Kerr from Simple Minds. The song may be overly sentimental, but at least it betrays some real emotions.

The album title came when Noel drunkenly misquoted Isaac Newtown's line, "If I have seen further, it is by standing on the shoulders of giants", from the side of the £2 coin, changing it for some reason to: standing on the *shoulder* of giants. Why no one told him it was grammatically incorrect is a mystery. The original title, however, was *Where Did it All Go Wrong*? Quite the existential question for one of the world's biggest rock stars. Whether Oasis were still the world's biggest band when the record was made is perhaps one of the key questions that sits at its heart. There was no denying the cultural impact the first two albums had on Britain and the world, but after the swerve off-piste that was *Be Here Now*, and the shifting of the music scene, Oasis had been relocated from the 'are great' zone to the 'were great' zone.

What made *Standing on the Shoulder of Giants* an interesting record was its saturation in the melancholia that made *OK Computer* and *Urban Hymns* such hits. Unfortunately, it didn't quite hit home because the sad-sack moniker was not one that fit Oasis as well as it did their contemporaries.

Noel attempted to emulate the bombastic, in-your-face rock 'n' roll that originally excited their audience on tracks like Put Yer Money Where Your Mouth Is and I Can See a Liar, but it is only on the more melancholic numbers that the album shows any real signs of their former brilliance. The eerie keyboards and angular guitars that accompany the intensity of Where

Did it All Go Wrong? – a track which also includes one of Noel's driest lyric to date: "Do you keep the receipts for the friends that you buy?" – clearly mine the darker side of his psyche. Meanwhile, album opener, the spirited instrumental Fuckin' in the Bushes, works hard at setting up an album that then never really gets going. The track eventually got the attention it deserved when film director Guy Ritchie used it in his 2000 boxing/crime caper *Snatch*.

The album's one moment of real excellence is Gas Panic!, where Noel finally laid out his fragile, post-drugs state of mind for all to see. As industrial, late Joy Division style machine samples clunk into place in the background, Gas Panic! opens with the line, "What tongue-less ghost of sin crept through my curtains?", a line swathed in gothic imagery worthy of Edgar Allan Poe, followed by the serpent-like alliteration of, "Sailing on a sea of sweat on a stormy night". And then, "I think he don't got a name but I can't be certain; And in me he starts to confide." The stanza, delivered by Liam in a voice so grizzled it forces the listener to strain to hear, is one of Noel's finest, its bleak, other-worldly narration influenced as much by gothic literature as any of his usual go-to artists, such as Bowie and even Kate Bush. The backing track is subtle and functional, finally launching into life at the beginning of the second verse as the guitars enter and the song kicks in proper, surprising the listener with how caught up in the moment they actually are.

The track was something of a highlight, not only on the album but also on the band's live set when they toured later in 2000, meriting its later inclusion on the live album, *Familiar to Millions*.

Before they could go on tour though, they needed another band member.

Despite playing bass in the video for Go Let It Out, Noel had no intention of remaining on bass duty long term, and so with the world tour for *Standing …* looming, the band needed to find a replacement for Guigsy. Help came in the equally likely and unlikely figure of Andy Bell. Another Creation alumnus, Bell's first band Ride had brought Alan McGee's former label some of its early mainstream success, their debut album *Nowhere* reaching number 11 in 1990, and their next two albums reaching number 5 in 1992 and 1994. After Ride split in 1996, Bell went on to form Hurricane #1, who had a semi-hit with the Step Into My World EP, which reached number 19 in October 1997. Then, as the band's second album loitered in the latter half of the chart in mid-1999, Bell quit the group, briefly joining indie-rock never-quite-weres Gay Dad in early 2000, before getting the call from Noel Gallagher. Bell hadn't played the bass before, but his guitar skills warranted the shift, and anyway, Noel thought he looked the part, so he was in.

Bell joined them on the *Standing …* tour, which began with their biggest run of dates in Japan, covering 29th February (leap year day) to 16th March. This was followed by France and Belgium between 21st and 25th March, and then on to America, where they played across the country between 5th and 29th April. The Noel-sung version of The Beatles' track Helter Skelter they performed at the Riverside Theatre in Milwaukee on 16th April made it on to the CD version of their live album *Familiar to Millions* as an added bonus.

The tour also included the recording of the video for their next single, Who Feels Love?, in Death Valley, California. This is the group's unabashed attempt at late sixties psychedelia, and owes a tremendous debt to Rain-era Beatles, as well as George Harrison's solo work, notably his 1971 *All Things Must Pass* debut.

Single 14:

Who Feels Love?
Released: 17th April 2000; UK Chart Position: 4; Label:
Big Brother; Album: *Standing on the Shoulder of Giants*
B-sides: One Way Road; Helter Skelter (Lennon and
McCartney)
Producers: Mark Stent, Noel Gallagher

The song features reversed guitar riffs and
sample loops, just as The Beatles pioneered back in 1966
on I'm Only Sleeping, and a semi-spiritual lyric.

Interestingly the line featuring the title says,
"Thank you for the sun, the one that shines on everyone
who feels love." Noel only turns it into a question for the
song's title. Again, hinting at his own state of mind.

UK Official Singles Chart – Top 10 – 23rd April 2000:

1. Toca's Miracle – Coco vs. Fragma
2. Fill Me In – Craig David
3. Thong Song – Sisqo
4. **Who Feels Love? – Oasis**
5. He Wasn't Man Enough – Toni Braxton
6. Buggin' Me – True Steppers ft. Dane Bowers
7. The Bad Touch – Bloodhound Gang
8. Flowers – Sweet Female Attitude
9. Private Emotion – Ricky Martin ft. Meja
10. Blow Ya Mind – Lock 'n' Load

Peaking at number 4, Who Feels Love? was
Oasis' first single not to reach the top 3 since October
1994, and the song spent just seven weeks on the chart
before dropping out, the inclusion of Helter Skelter on
the B-side not helping its success.

Single 15:

Sunday Morning Call
Released: 3rd July 2000; UK Chart Position: 4; Label:
Big Brother; Album: *Standing on the Shoulder of Giants*
B-sides: Carry Us All; Full On
Producers: Mark Stent, Noel Gallagher

Sunday Morning Call did not need to be released as a single, but the old Beatle work ethic of releasing a single every three months while touring an album was a tough one to shake. All the other tracks on the album were too dark for a summer release, so this was their only choice. It would be the last single from the band for nearly two years.

The song itself is listenable enough, with Noel taking the lead vocal (just his second on a single after Don't Look Back in Anger), and a gentle strummed acoustic giving way to an epic chorus that is immediately identifiable as Oasis.

UK Official Singles Chart – Top 10 – 9th July 2000:

1. Breathless – The Corrs
2. The Real Slim Shady – Eminem
3. Take a Look Around (Theme from MI2) – Limp Bizkit
4. Sunday Morning Call – Oasis
5. When I Said Goodbye/Summer of Love – Steps
6. Woman Trouble – Artful Dodger ft. Craig David
7. Will I Ever – Alice Deejay
8. Gotta Tell You – Samantha Mumba
9. Sandstorm – Darude
10. I Want Your Love – Atomic Kitten

There was a clear pattern developing in the charts that week. With The Corrs at number 1 with Breathless, Steps at 5 with When I Say Goodbye, Artful Dodger at 6, Samantha Mumba at 8, and Atomic Kitten at 10, pop music was experiencing something of a renaissance. Louise Wener says in *Live Forever* that British music defaults to pop for want of anything more solid, and this seemed to be happening in July 2000.

There were, however, hints of what was to come, with Eminem at 2 (down from 1) with the first single from his second album The Real Slim Shady. The popularity of rap music was on the rise in the UK, and soon Dr Dre, Snoop Dogg and Eminem's apprentice 50 Cent would all join him in the charts with solo singles, singles featuring each other, and their affiliated outfits (e.g. D-12), all selling by the bucket load.

This was nothing new – Oasis had fought it out in the charts in 1997 with Puff Daddy's mega hit I'll be Missing You – but it was a noticeable escalation; a sign of the dominance that hip-hop would soon have over the charts in the UK. To date, Eminem has had ten number 1 singles and ten number 1 albums in the UK.

Limp Bizkit were at 3 with Take a Look Around (Theme from MI2). The platinum-selling American rap/rock outfit had previously not made a dent in the UK charts, but this single marked the start of a run of seven top 20 singles and three top 10 albums. Limp Bizkit were the first nu-metal band to have a hit single in the UK, heralding the beginning of a short but powerful scene between 2000 and 2003 that saw the likes of Korn, The Deftones, Slipknot and Linkin Park all go mainstream in the UK.

Indie-rock music was not completely through though, and Oasis were not the last commercial indie band left in 2000. The week that Sunday Morning Call reached number 4, there was a single at number 11 (down from 4) called Yellow, the second single proper from Coldplay.

This began a decade-long string of ten singles to reach the top 10, including two number 1s, plus eight number 1 albums. Heavily influenced by Oasis, despite claims from Liam that they looked like geography teachers, Coldplay took over Oasis' mantel as the most commercially successful indie-rock band in the UK.

Live Album:

Familiar to Millions
Released: 13th November 2000; UK Chart Position: 5; Label: Big Brother
Track Listing: Fuckin' in the Bushes; Go Let it Out; Who Feels Love?; Supersonic; Shakermaker; Acquiesce; Step Out; Gas Panic!; Roll With It; Stand by Me; Wonderwall; Cigarettes & Alcohol; Don't Look Back in Anger; Live Forever; Hey Hey, My My (Into the Black) [Young]; Champagne Supernova; Rock 'n' Roll Star; (Helter Skelter) [Lennon, McCartney]
Producers: Mark Stent, Paul Stacey

UK Official Albums Chart – Top 10 – 19th November 2000:

1. *1* – The Beatles
2. *Coast to Coast* – Westlife
3. *The Greatest Hits* – Texas
4. *Buzz* – Steps
5. **Familiar to Millions – Oasis**
6. *Parachutes* – Coldplay
7. *One Night Only: The Greatest Hits* – Elton John
8. *Born to Do It* – Craig David
9. *Sing When You're Winning* – Robbie Williams
10. *All That You Can't Leave Behind* – U2

Oasis' first live performance DVD/VHS to be released since *There and Then* in 1996, the arrogantly but accurately named *Familiar to Millions* was also released on CD, reaching number 5 in the UK Official Albums Chart in November 2000. This was their only live album.

Contrary to previous pre-Christmas album charts, this one was not packed with best-ofs, with just three in the top 10, and 10 in the top 40. The top 10 was still made up of some of the most successful acts of the time though. Aside from The Beatles, Elton John, Oasis, Robbie Williams, U2 and Coldplay, Westlife would go on to become one of the most successful boybands of all time, with 14 UK number 1 singles and eight number 1 albums.

(Not so) Familiar

The live album was Oasis' first chance to show everyone what Oasis 2.0 looked and sounded like on stage. Gem Archer and Andy Bell had taken over from Bonehead and Guigsy, but their roles within the band had developed to accommodate their advanced musicianship. Where Bonehead strummed the chords, Archer fills in Noel's guitar licks during Don't Look Back in Anger. And Bell – reeling from the Noel-led chant of "Who the fuck is Andy Bell?" – plays his bass like a lead guitar, including the much more prominent lines Noel played on the *Standing* … material, most notably on Go Let it Out and Who Feels Love? The band had evolved, and it brought them a new lease of life.

Knowing their audience, they chose to stick predominantly to the early material, bringing back old favourites Shakermaker and Cigarettes and Alcohol, as well as dusting off some classic material that had not seen the light of day before, such as Step Out. Knowing full well what a cliché it had become, the stool and acoustic section is now gone, eliminating the likes of Cast No Shadow and The Masterplan, and meaning Wonderwall is now played on an electric guitar. Old favourites such as Champagne Supernova and Live Forever sound as glorious as ever though.

Noel also adds the Neil Young song Hey Hey, My My (Into the Black) to his repertoire; the song famed for being quoted by Kurt Cobain in his suicide note ("It's better to burn out than to fade away") Noel dedicated the song to Cobain.

This was also the last concert played by a British band at the old Wembley Stadium (Bon Jovi were the last to play there a couple of weeks later). With just a handful of dates before the tour finished a month later, the concert on 21st July 2000 has something of an end of term feel about it. Liam, on prime obnoxious form as he demands that women bare their breasts on the screen, later acknowledges what a weird year it has been. Perhaps he is referring to the lack of drugs ingested on the tour.

The band finish with Rock 'n' Roll Star, a track they hadn't played live for several years. While a song about a band wanting to be rock stars played by a band who were rock stars could have sounded trite, lines like, "Look at you now you're all in my hands tonight", took on another resonance, adding an element of nostalgia as the new line-up finished out the era of the old one.

The song bookends the band's first phase, providing an apt stopping point as it harks back to their old days. The end of the Wembley concert is not necessarily the sign of a new beginning, but it certainly provides a full stop for this chapter.

CHAPTER EIGHT
Heathen Chemistry: The Elder Statesmen (2001-2003)

After the intense flurry of their first five years, the next eight years were somewhat contained in comparison for Oasis. With their new line-up, and their new label, they slipped seamlessly into the role of rock behemoth. As can be seen in the 2007 tourumentary *Lord Don't Slow Me Down*, world tours became a blur of blank arenas, faceless dressing rooms, hotel rooms, hotel bars, and underground car parks where fleets of FBI-style 4x4 vans would whisk them off to the next city for the whole process to begin again. Separating the band from their fans and keeping them away from anything that might be seen as exciting or interesting in the cities they were playing seemed to be paramount. Touring became a trip down a bland 21st century high street flanked by endless Starbucks and McDonalds.

The banal routine of touring aside, in many ways this was a golden era for the band. Despite his continued outbursts at whatever was annoying him that week, Liam seemed to have been chilled by age and fatherhood, so the band could focus on creating music. By the time their last album *Dig Out Your Soul* was released in 2008, there were few surprises left that the band could offer the world. But, like many acts entering middle-age, creating music for themselves and the people who loved them had become more important than kicking up a storm.

Between 2001 and 2008, they released three studio albums and 11 singles, as well as holding an annual world tour, and they – and their fans – seemed content with this.

The second half of January 2001 saw a string of South American dates complete the *Standing on the Shoulder of Giants* world tour. By May they were back on the road in America with the Black Crowes and Spacehog, on what imaginatively became known as the Tour of Brotherly Love, due to all three bands featuring a pair of bickering brothers.

After a further string of UK dates, the band were finally back in the studio in October to record what would become their fifth studio album, *Heathen Chemistry*. The music was recorded relatively quickly, with the instrumentation finished by the end of the year, but it then took Liam three months to record his vocals. This meant the album's release date was pushed back to 1st July 2002, more than two years since the release of their last album. The length of recording threw up another issue that the band had not had to contend with before – tracks being released illegally on the internet. By the time they came to play live, and before the record was even released, fans knew the words to many of the songs.

Heathen Chemistry is a competent album by most standards, but Oasis were not like most bands. It's difficult to judge their work on its own terms at this stage in their career, but it's obvious the band had made real attempts to develop their sound. Noel wrote six and a half of the 11 tracks, with Liam down for two and a half, and Gem and Andy one each, giving the record a bit of distance from the band's previous output.

Archer and Bell were both singers and guitarists, but the band are careful to stick to the familiar line-up from *Familiar to Millions*, with Noel playing lead guitar and providing backing vocals, anchoring their sound within the confines of what the audience expected. The churning, barre chord heavy rock tracks are immediately identifiable as Oasis, but the effortlessness of each composition gives the album a confident lack of urgency. The band clearly have nothing to prove and are relaxed with their position in the rock pantheon.

It is the band's only album to be completely self-produced.

Single 16:

The Hindu Times
Released: 15th April 2002; UK Chart Position: 1; Label:
Big Brother; Album: *Heathen Chemistry*
B-sides: Just Getting Older; Idler's Dream
Producers: Oasis

With a title taken from a T-shirt logo, album opener and lead single The Hindu Times is classic Oasis. Propelled by a distinct George Harrison-esque guitar riff, the song appears to be about nothing more than what its key line suggests, with Liam demanding, "God give me some of that rock 'n' roll!" and, "I get so high I just can't feel it."

UK Official Singles Chart – Top 10 – 21st April 2002:

1. **The Hindu Times – Oasis**
2. Girlfriend – NSYNC
3. There Goes the Fear – Doves
4. Unchained Melody – Gareth Gates
5. Lazy – X-Press 2 ft. David Byrne
6. Whenever Wherever – Shakira
7. How You Remind Me – Nickelback
8. 4 My People – Missy Elliott
9. I'm Not a Girl, Not Yet a Woman – Britney Spears
10. Me Julie – Ali G and Shaggy

The Hindu Times went straight in at number 1, with the first single from the second album by Doves at number 3. They were part of a contingent of new

Manchester bands beginning to find success that also included Elbow, I Am Kloot and Badly Drawn Boy, who all rose to prominence by partly trading on hometown heroes like The Smiths and New Order.

Gareth Gates was at number 4 (down from 1) with his version of Unchained Melody. He found fame on the first season of *Pop Idol*, his success marking the beginning of a slew of Simon Cowell reality TV show contestants who dominated the charts (particularly at Christmas) over the next ten years. Gates, an inoffensive cruise ship style crooner, brought once famous songs to fans of middle-of-the-road music across Britain, just as Cowell had done with Robson and Jerome five years earlier. Gates even sang the same song as R&J.

Mike Skinner, aka The Streets, had a new entry at number 30 with Let's Push Things Forward. Skinner noted on the song, his second single, how placid and pedestrian the music in the charts had become, asking the nation to push things forward.

There was also a smattering in the lower reaches of the top 100 of acts like The Vines, The White Stripes, Ryan Adams and The Electric Soft Parade, who would come to define the next movement in indie-rock music: the garage-rock revival.

Single 17:

Stop Crying Your Heart Out
Released: 17th June 2002; UK Chart Position: 2; Label: Big Brother; Album: *Heathen Chemistry*
B-sides: Thank You for the Good Times (Bell); Shout It Out Loud
Producers: Oasis

Few modern rockers can tweak the heart strings with a rock ballad quite like Noel Gallagher. His work falls on just the right side of sentimental, so that butch lads from Essex can singalong live then shed a tear quietly at home. The second single from *Heathen Chemistry*, Stop Crying Your Heart Out, has an understated elegance, built from a simple piano line, making it one of the band's best examples of restraint.

UK Official Singles Chart – Top 10 – 23rd June 2002:

1. A Little Less Conversation – Elvis vs. JXL
2. **Stop Crying Your Heart Out – Oasis**
3. When You Look at Me – Christina Milian
4. Hot in Here – Nelly
5. The Logical Song – Scooter
6. Here – Chad Kroeger ft. Josey Scott
7. Roll On/This is How We Do It – Mis-teeq
8. Love at First Sight – Kylie Minogue
9. Without Me – Eminem
10. Just a Little – Liberty X

If you're going to be kept from the top spot, then there are few acts better to take second place to than Elvis, who was back at number 1, 25 years after he died, with a remix of A Little Less Conversation. The King prevented Oasis from reaching the top spot with the second single from *Heathen Chemistry*, the excellent Stop Crying Your Heart Out.

The resurgence in quality British indie-rock was also still going strong, with the likes of Athlete, Badly Drawn Boy and Idlewild all in the top 100.

The Hindu Times gives way to Force of Nature, a vaguely bar room brawl-esque number – with added honky-tonk piano – which is something of a precursor to The Importance of Being Idle, the number 1 single from 2005's *Don't Believe the Truth*.

Album 5:

Heathen Chemistry
Released: 1st July 2002; UK Chart Position: 1; Label:
Big Brother
Track Listing: The Hindu Times; Force of Nature;
Hung in a Bad Place (Archer); Stop Crying Your Heart
Out; Songbird (L Gallagher); Little by Little; A Quick
Peep (Bell); (Probably) All in the Mind; She is Love;
Born on a Different Cloud (L Gallagher); Better Man
(L Gallagher/N Gallagher); The Cage
Producers: Oasis

When not ripping themselves off, Oasis were
clearly still happy to crib from other acts (the intro to
Force of Nature is lifted directly from Nightclubbing by
Iggy Pop), and the album's next track, Gem Archer's
Hung in a Bad Place, borrows another Iggy riff, this time
the Stooges' No Fun, famously played by The Sex Pistols
at their last concert (before reforming) at the Winterland
in San Francisco in January 1978. Hung in a Bad Place is
a solid punk-rock track, brought to life by Liam's snarled
vocal, but one that may well not have made the cut back
in 1995.

Lifting bits and pieces from rock history,
including their own back catalogue, was nothing new for
Oasis. Noel had always happily worn his influences on his
sleeve, a move that worked in his favour as often as it
didn't. He would include lines from the same songs he
was lifting chord structures and melodies from, à la Hello
from *(What's the Story) Morning Glory?*, which keeps in the
line "It's good to be back" from Gary Glitter's original;
just as Put Yer Money Where Your Mouth Is, from
Standing on the Shoulder of Giants, includes the line: "... and
your hands upon the wheel," lifted directly from The

Doors track Roadhouse Blues, a song that it sounds remarkably similar to.

Despite this perennial Oasis issue, *Heathen Chemistry* is packed with solid belters that sit comfortably alongside some of the band's best loved songs. As the years passed by, it became clear that no British band since The Beatles could match Oasis for consistently producing such listenable material, a space that none of their successors – the likes of Kasabian, The Courteeners or even The Arctic Monkeys – ever managed to adequately fill. The only other band to come close has been Coldplay, but few people seem proud to call themselves a Coldplay fan, however good their music is. As the comedian Nish Kumar has it, "The Problem with being in Coldplay, is that people HATE Coldplay."

UK Official Albums Chart – Top 10 – 7th July 2002:

1. ***Heathen Chemistry* – Oasis**
2. *Nellyville* – Nelly
3. *The Eminem Show* – Eminem
4. *Greatest Hits I, II & III* – Queen
5. *Read My Lips* – Sophie Ellis Bextor
6. *Fever* – Kylie Minogue
7. *Charango* – Morcheeba
8. *Escape* – Enrique Iglesias
9. *No Angel* – Dido
10. *Hullaboloo* – Muse

Heathen Chemistry was a huge success, going straight in at the top spot, spending nine weeks in the top 10 and a further 31 weeks in the top 100. It went three times platinum in the UK, selling more than a million copies, and an estimated 3.5m worldwide, making it their fifth most successful studio album.

The coolest band in the UK at this time were The Strokes, the uber-stylish New York outfit who were at the forefront of the garage-rock revival scene, and who the *NME* were heralding as the saviours of music. Such was the demand to see them play when they arrived in the UK in the summer of 2001 that they were promoted from the second stage to the main stage at the Reading Festival, in case 50,000 people attempted to ram themselves into a tent meant for two thousand. They had released just one single at the time. Their debut album *Is This It* was one of the most hotly anticipated releases of the decade, so it shocked no one when it reached number 2 in September 2001. They were prevented from reaching the top spot by another American genre band, nu-metal outfit Slipknot and their debut *Iowa*.

The Strokes' UK counterparts were The Libertines, who released their first single, What a Waster, on 12ᵗʰ June 2002. Their first album *Up the Bracket* became an instant classic when released in November, and by the time their second, self-titled album reached the top spot in September 2004, they had already exploded in a haze of drug-fuelled mayhem that even Liam Gallagher would baulk at. Despite co-singer Pete Doherty being jailed for burgling co-singer Carl Barât's flat, the band managed to release their number 1 eponymous album in August 2004 before disintegrating less than a year later, a sad state of affairs for a talented band with so much to offer. The Libertines eventually reformed in 2009 and released their long-awaited third album, *Anthems for a Doomed Youth*, in 2016. At the time of writing, they are still enjoying their new lease of life.

Many of the best garage rock groups were imported: The White Stripes, The Von Bondies, The Yeah Yeah Yeahs, Interpol and The Black Rebel Motorcycle Club were all from America; The Hives and The Soundtrack of Our Lives hailed from Sweden; The Datsuns were from New Zealand; and The Vines were from Australia. Unlike Britpop, it was a scene with no borders, as long as you were happy to travel to the UK and sing in English.

Among the new wave of Manchester bands, Elbow, Doves and Badly Drawn Boy all released excellent records between 2000 and 2003. Elbow are still going strong after releasing their ninth studio album in October 2019. They won the Mercury Music Prize with 2008's *The Seldom Seen Kid*, an award that Badly Drawn Boy also picked up for his debut *The Hour of the Bewilderbeast* in 2000. Doves were also nominated that year, as were Coldplay and former Verve singer Richard Ashcroft.

After a few years in the doldrums, it seemed that Britain was experiencing another golden age of music. This was the environment that Oasis released *Heathen Chemistry* into: a reinvigorated UK music scene, producing some of its best music for years. Although the bands in the early 2000s didn't quite reach the level of chart dominance that the Britpop bands had in the mid-90s, their more serious approach to music gave them greater longevity.

Single 18:

Little By Little/She is Love
Released: 23rd September 2002; UK Chart Position: 2;
Label: Big Brother; Album: *Heathen Chemistry*
B-sides: My Generation (The Who)
Producers: Oasis

Featuring a cover of The Who classic My Generation as a supporting third track, the double A-side released on 23rd September 2002 was the third single from *Heathen Chemistry*, and featured Noel singing lead on both of the main tracks. It was the first time Oasis had released a double A-side, a trick that was much more prominent in the sixties and seventies, before CDs made it possible to have more than two tracks on a single. The Beatles, weighed down with so many potential singles, often chose to release double A-sides, the most famous being Penny Lane/Strawberry Fields Forever, released in February 1967; the first Beatles single not to reach number 1 since Please, Please Me in January 1963.

Little by Little was a fairly obvious choice of single, its acoustic led verse giving way to an anthemic chorus that fans delighted in singing along to live (the track later became Noel's daughter Anais' favourite), but choosing She is Love as the other A-side comes from slightly left-field. The acoustic track, which shares something of an identity with It's Better People from the Roll With It single, is about Noel's girlfriend, later his second wife, Sara MacDonald. The title says it all really.

UK Official Singles Chart – Top 10 – 7th July 2002:

1. The Long and Winding Road/Suspicious – Gareth Gates and Will Young
2. **Little By Little/She is Love – Oasis**
3. Complicated – Avril Lavigne
4. Just Like a Pill – Pink
5. The Tide is High – Atomic Kitten
6. Gangsta Lovin – Eve ft. Alicia Keys
7. What I Go to School For – Busted
8. Cleaning Out My Closet – Eminem
9. Strange and Beautiful – Aqualung
10. Nessaja – Scooter

The band were in the midst of the *Heathen Chemistry* tour when the single was released and peaked at number 2 in the charts, taking second place to the joint release from Will Young and Gareth Gates of The Beatles' The Long and Winding Road (which was never released as a single by the Fab Four).

Young and Gates came first and second on *Pop Idol* in 2001, and their continuing popularity showcased the growing chart dominance of reality TV show contestants. Shows like *Pop Idol* and *X Factor* seemed like a short cut to fame for many fledgling singers, but many didn't bank on how fickle it could be. Gates released three albums between 2002 and 2007, with decreasing levels of success, the first peaking at number 1, the second number 11, and the third number 23.

Young, however, was one of the few solo success stories from the reality crowd, chiefly because he claimed an identity for himself early on and released work that he liked, rather than what Simon Cowell thought people wanted to buy. He has released eight albums to date, the most recent being *Lexicon*, which reached number 2 in July 2019.

Single 19:

Songbird
Released: 3rd February 2003; UK Chart Position: 3;
Label: Big Brother; Album: *Heathen Chemistry*
B-sides: (You've Got) The Heart of a Star (L Gallagher); Columbia (live)
Producers: Oasis

The first single released by the band not composed by Noel was Songbird, Liam Gallagher's ode to girlfriend and future wife Nicole Appleton. The mother of Liam's second child, Gene, Appleton came to fame as one of the members of All Saints, who had a string of hits in the late nineties. After All Saints split in 2001, she became one half of Appleton with her sister Natalie, and the pair had a couple of hits at the tail end of 2002 and beginning of 2003. Natalie is married to the other Liam of nineties British music, Liam Howlett from the Prodigy.

Songbird, similar in style if not tone to She is Love, is a simple acoustic number that features Liam on guitar, with Noel on piano, and Gem Archer on that underused pop instrument, the harmonium.

UK Official Singles Chart – Top 10 – 9th February 2003:

1. All the Things She Said – Tatu
2. Cry Me a River – Justin Timberlake
3. **Songbird – Oasis**
4. Stole – Kelly Rowland
5. Gimme the Light – Sean Paul
6. Lose Yourself – Eminem
7. OK – Big Bruvaz
8. Stop Living the Lie – David Sneddon
9. 03 Bonnie & Clyde – Jazy-Z ft. Beyonce Knowles
10. The Year 3000 – Busted

Hip-hop was still on its way to domination, with five of the top 10 singles. Symbolically, the chart featured the first collaboration between the future king and queen of hip-hop Jay-Z and Beyonce (who would marry five years later in 2008), as well as the ever-present Eminem, whose single Lose Yourself was down from the top spot five weeks previously. Reality star David Sneddon from *Fame Academy* (which was pitched as a more highbrow version of Pop Idol because the contestants all lived together in a retreat and wrote their own songs) was at 8, down from 1.

Oasis' only release in 2003, Songbird was released two days before the band returned to the Point in Dublin for two nights, their first dates in Ireland since July 2000, and their first gigs at this venue since their heroic "homecoming" in 1996. The *Heathen Chemistry* tour ended with four nights in Germany, leaving the band pretty much semi-retired until June 2004 when they emerged to play Glastonbury. Their next new music was Lyla, the first single from their sixth studio album *Don't Believe the Truth*, in May 2005.

With the press no longer camped out on their doorsteps, Oasis were much freer than they had been before. No longer hampered by the ridiculous levels of hype and attention that had clung to them during *Be Here Now* and *Standing on the Shoulder of Giants*, they could now be judged for the music.

They had moved away from producing photocopies of Beatles' lyrics and, with four songwriters at their disposal, were free to explore more interesting ground. In many ways, the next few years of Oasis' career were their most fruitful. The three albums they released were not their most popular or their most pored over, but this brought much-needed space for the listener to discover new things about them. They are the gift that keeps on giving, even today.

CHAPTER NINE
Don't Believe the Truth: Rediscovered Riches (2004-2005)

Don't Believe the Truth was released on 30th May 2005 and quickly became Oasis' most successful record since *Be Here Now*. The band, previously impervious to changing musical movements, were about to understand how waiting to release the right product at the right time could change fortunes.

By 2005, the garage-rock revival scene was well past its peak. The Strokes' second album, 2003's *Room on Fire*, had been extremely underwhelming; The White Stripes were past their commercial prime; The Libertines had split; and the likes of The Yeah Yeah Yeahs, The Von Bondies and The Liars had all scuttled back across the Atlantic. Only Kings of Leon, previously championed by Noel Gallagher, seemed to cross the terrain between garage-rock and indie-rock, and their second album *Aha Shake Heartbreak* reached number 3 in February 2005.

As 2005 wore on, the most successful British band since Oasis came to light; their influences lying not in the garages of Seattle, but in the spit-stained basements of the North. By February 2006, Sheffield's Arctic Monkeys boasted two number 1 singles (October 2005's I Bet You Look Good on the Dancefloor, and January 2006's When the Sun Goes Down), and their debut album, *Whatever People Say I Am That's What I'm Not*, became the quickest selling debut ever in late January 2006 (taking over from Elastica, who took over from Oasis).

Arctic Monkeys leader Alex Turner's lyrical talent might have more in common with English novelists and playwrights from the fifties and sixties such as Alan Sillitoe (the name of the band's debut album was taken from the 1960 film version of Sillitoe's *Saturday Night, Sunday Morning*, staring the prototype working-class rebel Albert Finney), but Turner shared a certain dry northern humour with Noel and Liam which he transferred to his lyrics ("the weekend rock stars are in the toilets, practising their lines"). As well as the Gallaghers, the music press also drew comparisons between Turner and Paul Weller's early incarnation with The Jam. The Arctic Monkeys' appearance on the scene was as exciting as The Sex Pistols and The Clash in 1977, Weller and The Jam in 1978, and Oasis in 1994, and their success filled a vacant slot at the top of the charts for an intelligent working-class band who wrote simple but infectious rock 'n' roll tunes.

With garage rock dead (or dormant), and the success of the Arctic Monkeys growing, many saw 2005 as the second wave of Britpop, and guitar bands such as Stereophonics, Razorlight, Editors, Kaiser Chiefs, Pigeon Detectives, The Enemy and Elbow all experienced huge commercial success. Even electro-indie pioneers New Order released two albums of indie-rock music dominated by Oasis style guitar riffs: 2001's *Get Ready* (the video for lead single Crystal featured a fictious band called The Killers – who would in turn give their name to the American band that released one of the decade's best-loved albums, *Hot Fuss*), and 2005's *Waiting for the Siren's Call.*

Whether Oasis were considered part of this second wave of Britpop or not, they were key influencers, and the time was ripe for their return.

The initial sessions for *Don't Believe the Truth* took place in December 2003, while Alan White was still the band's drummer. After being accused of not taking his role seriously enough, Alan acrimoniously left the group in January 2004. He had occupied the drum stool since April 1995; nearly nine years. His replacement came in the form of rock royalty, Zak Starkey, son of Beatle Ringo Starr, who had cut his chops drumming for The Who. Zak never joined the band full time, but did play on their final two albums, as well as playing live until December 2007. His work was supplemented by Terry Kirkbride formerly of Proud Mary, who played on Mucky Fingers. Kirkbride later played live for Noel Gallagher's High Flying Birds.

Death in Vegas leader Richard Fearless was the first producer to attempt a session with Oasis in January for *Don't Believe* ... but his work was all but disowned and the sessions deemed not up to par. The next set of sessions in February, now with Zak on drums and Noel as producer, were dumped for the same reason, giving the band a few months off to work on their song writing. After headlining that year's Glastonbury Festival – sharing headlining duties with Sir Paul McCartney and Muse – they showcased two new songs, neither written by Noel: The Meaning of Soul, penned by Liam; and A Bell Will Ring, written by Gem Archer.

Playing live renewed their drive to create the new album and, by the end of year, they were in LA, Noel having magnanimously handed over the producing role to American Dave Sardy. This was the beginning of a long relationship between the band and Sardy, who would also go on to produce their final album *Dig Out Your Soul*, and co-produce Noel's first solo album, *Noel Gallagher's High Flying Birds*, in 2011.

Single 20:

Lyla
Released: 16th May 2005; UK Chart Position: 1; Label: Big Brother; Album: *Don't Believe the Truth*
B-sides: Eyeball Tickler (Archer); Won't Let You Down (L Gallagher)
Producers: Dave Sardy, Noel Gallagher

Oasis announced their return to the scene with the rabble-rousing single Lyla. A close cousin to the Rolling Stones' Street Fighting Man, Lyla is a classic earworm that picks up where The Hindu Times left off. The track was written by Noel around the time of *Heathen Chemistry* and was dug up when Sony BMG told the band there was a lack of releasable singles on the new album.

The band, keen to release a crafted album rather than just a collection of potential singles, were reluctant to include Lyla. Ultimately, the decision to put it out caused a rift between record company and band that led to them choosing not to renew their contract when it expired at the end of 2006.

Despite the reticence, the single was a huge success, and went straight in at number 1 on its release in May 2005.

UK Official Singles Chart – Top 10 – 22nd May 2005:

1. **Lyla – Oasis**
2. Lonely – Akon
3. Don't Phunk with my Heart – Black Eyed Peas
4. Feel Good Inc. – Gorillaz
5. (Is This the Way To) Amarillo – Tony Christie ft. Peter Kay
6. Hold You Down – Jennifer Lopez ft. Fat Joe
7. Hate It or Love It – Game ft. 50 Cent
8. Signs – Snoop Dogg/Wilson/Timberlake
9. Owner of a Lonely Heart – Max Graham vs. Yes
10. Everyday I Love You Less and Less – Kaiser Chiefs

The Gallaghers' old sparring partner Damon Albarn from Blur was at 4 (down from 2) with the classic Gorillaz track Feel Good Inc. With Blur on hiatus, Albarn began Gorillaz as a dance/rock/hip-hop side project in 2001, but after the phenomenal success of the first album he delved further into the experimental side of his developing musicality on the second album. Feel Good Inc. was the first single released from *Demon Days*, perfectly capturing the pinnacle of accessible experimentation reached by Albarn in his work with Gorillaz. Today, Gorillaz are synonymous with progressive electronic world music, and their tracks have featured guests as varied as Bobby Womack and Peter Hook. Albarn had come a long way from Country House, but how far had Oasis come in comparison? It was a complicated question.

Album 6:

Don't Believe the Truth
Released: 30th May 2005; UK Chart Position: 1; Label: Big Brother
Track Listing: Turn Up the Sun (Bell); Mucky Fingers; Lyla; Love Like a Bomb (L Gallagher/Archer); The Importance of Being Idle; The Meaning of Soul (L Gallagher); Guess God Thinks I'm Abel (L Gallagher); Part of the Queue; Keep the Dream Alive (Bell); A Bell Will Ring (Archer); Let There Be Love
Producers: Dave Sardy, Noel Gallagher

With just five of the 11 tracks written by Noel, *Don't Believe the Truth* was Oasis' most collaborative album, taking what they started on *Heathen Chemistry* and shifting it up a notch. Liam, in particular, seemed to be coming into his own, writing three of the tracks (one with Gem Archer), while Archer got solo credit for another song, and Andy Bell for two more, including the epic opening track, Turn Up the Sun.

Arguably the strongest composition on the album, Turn Up the Sun slowly works its way into life with layered jangling guitars reminiscent of Bell's former group Ride (whose success for Creation Records had, in part, made Oasis' career possible), before the huge wall of guitars, at once Oasis, signal the song has begun proper. The simplicity of the chord sequence, anchored in Bm and dropping to a satisfying Gmajor in the chorus, is familiar from early Oasis songs such as Columbia, but is perhaps more reminiscent of Bell's time as one of the key players in the shoegazing movement.

The band also switched instruments, with Noel finally foregoing his lead guitar in favour of Bell and Archer. Like *Definitely Maybe*, the album has no keyboards or programming, giving it a more open, freer sound, but also meaning the tracks ran the risk of sounding disjointed when put together. If Noel was worried that the inclusion of an obvious single like Lyla might highlight a lack of consistency, then Sardy's involvement was paramount. His mix kept the songs sonically linked, with many taking on an early seventies *Let it Bleed*-era Rolling Stones acoustic sound, like Liam's Love Like a Bomb – a rare Oasis track set in 6/8 time – and Noel's The Importance of Being Idle, which owed a debt to The Kinks' Sunny Afternoon and Dead End Street.

Sardy maintains control by keeping the tracks compressed but not constricted, typified by his decision to bookend the huge guitars on Turn Up the Sun with the delicate piano chords of Let There be Love. Where Owen Morris' (and Noel's) work on *Morning Glory* produced an album that is always at the front of the speakers (and the mind), *Don't Believe* ... was more subtle. Perhaps surprisingly, with three guitarists, the songs have fewer layers than previous albums, affording them space.

Most importantly, the band's chemistry had developed, and the album was a marked return to the confidence of their *Morning Glory* era. The record chimed with the public and signalled another hugely fruitful period. *Don't Believe* ... remained on the chart for 41 weeks, slotting itself into the top spot ahead of Gorillaz second album *Demon Days*. It was like the old days, when Oasis and Blur battled it out for top spot.

<u>UK Official Albums Chart – Top 10 – 5th June 2005:</u>

1. ***Don't Believe the Truth* – Oasis**
2. *Demon Days* – Gorillaz
3. *Forever Faithless: The Greatest Hits* – Faithless
4. *Monkey Business* – Black Eyed Peas
5. *Back to Bedlam* – James Blunt
6. *Love Angel Music Baby* – Gwen Stefani
7. *Employment* – Kaiser Chiefs
8. *Trouble* – Akon
9. *Jackinabox* – Turin Breaks
10. *Eye to the Telescope* – KT Tunstall

The *Don't Believe the Truth* world tour began at the Astoria in Central London on 10th May 2005, a week before Lyla was released, and ran until the end of March 2006 in Central America. This whole period was captured on film for the tourumentary *Lord Don't Slow Me Down*, released in October 2007 alongside the band's first (and only) download-only single of the same name. The film portrayed Oasis as the elder statesmen of rock, relaxed in the lofty position they now found themselves in, and enjoying a return to the fortunes they last saw in their early days.

The band and critics alike toyed with the idea that the album was as good as *Definitely Maybe*. But, while it was definitely a return to form, the two albums remain incomparable. Where *Definitely Maybe* has an urgent, naïve nihilism, *Don't Believe the Truth* is considered, well-honed and temperate. It is the sound of a band made wealthy by their music, producing music with well-tuned ears, not because they have to, but because they want to.

This tour marked the start of Oasis' relationship with Kasabian, who supported them alongside the

Australian rock band, Jet. Even before the support slot, Kasabian had been labelled as the likely successors to Oasis in the UK music scene; the rising future champs sparring with the big boys. The Leicester band released their eponymous debut album in September 2004. It went straight into an indie-rock filled top 10 at number 4, below Keane's *Hopes and Fears* at 3, above Razorlight's *Up All Night* at 5, and keeping company with eponymous albums by The Libertines at number 6 and Franz Ferdinand at 10.

Since 1997, Kasabian had been fronted by outgoing singer Tom Meighan and quiet guitarist Serge Pizzorno, a dynamic they shared with Liam and Noel. Combining this with their tendency toward the outspoken and their ability to pen anthemic crowd-pleasing tunes, meant they were quickly lumped into the Oasis category by music critics. Far from producing straightforward rock 'n' roll though, *Kasabian* is packed with keyboards, synthesisers and sample loops, as well as indie guitars. Their music is a strange hybrid of indie-dance-rock, as heavily influenced by Donna Summer as Oasis.

The *Don't Believe* … tour clearly had a big impact on Kasabian, and by 2006 their second album, the aptly named *Empire*, propelled them into the big league. Where *Kasabian* had more introspective material such as I.D., its follow-up was anthem after anthem. *Empire* and its four follow ups all went straight in at number 1 in the album charts.

Oasis' most idiosyncratic single, The Importance of Being Idle, is an autobiographical story by Noel about his growing feeling that his days of incredible song writing proficiency are now well behind him. It was the band's final number 1 single, spending a solid 22 weeks on the chart.

Single 21:

The Importance of Being Idle
Released: 22nd August 2005; UK Chart Position: 1;
Label: Big Brother; Album: *Don't Believe the Truth*
B-sides: Pass Me Down the Wine (L Gallagher); The
Quiet Ones (Archer)
Producers: Dave Sardy, Noel Gallagher

UK Official Singles Chart – Top 10 – 28th August 2005:

1. **The Importance of Being Idle – Oasis**
2. Pon De Replay – Rhianna
3. Bad Day – Daniel Powter
4. Lay Your Hands – Simon Webbe
5. You're Beautiful – James Blunt
6. Don't Lie – Black Eyed Peas
7. Long Hot Summer – Girls Aloud
8. I'll Be Ok – McFly
9. I Predict a Riot/Sink That Ship – Kaiser Chiefs
10. Your Doorbell – The White Stripes

Single 22:

Let There Be Love
Released: 28th November 2005; UK Chart Position: 2;
Label: Big Brother; Album: *Don't Believe the Truth*
B-sides: Sittin' Here in Silence (On My Own); Rock 'n'
Roll Star (live – City of Manchester Stadium, 2nd July
2005)
Producers: Dave Sardy, Noel Gallagher

UK Official Singles Chart – Top 10 – 4th December 2005:

1. Stickwitu – Pussycat Dolls
2. **Let There Be Love – Oasis**
3. Hung Up – Madonna
4. You Raise Me Up - Westlife
5. My Humps – Black Eyed Peas
6. No Worries – Simon Webbe
7. Because of You – Kelly Clarkson
8. Albion – Babyshambles
9. Biology – Girls Aloud
10. Dirty Harry - Gorillaz

Oasis always had a tumultuous time at the Q Awards, held annually in October. Noel, high on … life, cornered Tony Blair in 1995, and, in 1998, Liam was arrested for cocaine possession, but in 2005 they were the life and soul of the party when they won both the People's Choice Awards, the only award voted for by the people; and best album for *Don't Believe The Truth*, capping off what was becoming an excellent year. Noel thanked all the girls in the office for voting for the People's Choice Award, but was clearly pretty chuffed with receiving both, and the kudos that went along with them.

Then the band were back on the road again in Europe, Japan, Australia, and finishing the year back in the UK. This meant they were in the midst of an Australian tour when Let There Be Love, the third and final single from *Don't Believe* … went to number 2 in the UK Official Singles Chart at the end of November 2005.

The song, Oasis' most schmaltzy single to date, is a gentle ode to love itself in "a world come undone at the seams." A classic duet between the Gallagher brothers, with Liam taking the verse and chorus and Noel the middle-eight, the song dates back to the *Standing on the Shoulder of Giants* period, which explains its self-reflective lyric.

CHAPTER TEN
Dig Out Your Soul: The End is Nigh (2006-2008)

The *Don't Believe the Truth* world tour rolled on into 2006, with a run of European dates before the band headed first to the Far East – Thailand, South Korea and Singapore – and then South America and Mexico, finishing up in the USA at the end of March. After another prolonged break, the band once again appeared at the Q Awards in October, winning Best Live Act in the World Today. A slightly uncomfortable win seeing as Noel had previously dismissed the live award was a token win, with the line: "Whoop-de-doo, you can play the guitar!"

Noel also won the Classic Songwriter award, and performed solo at the Union Chapel for charity Mencap at the end of October, and Cabert Sauvage in Paris. He had also performed solo at the Wadsworth Theatre in LA on 9th October (John Lennon's birthday). The sets consisted of Oasis songs and Beatles covers, and the LA gig included a version of Whatever played in the style of Bob Dylan's Subterranean Homesick Blues, dedicated to the man himself. With Noel no longer playing his acoustic sets live with the band, these concerts provided his major acoustic outlet away from Oasis.

In November 2006 the band's first best-of album was released by Sony, completing their contractual obligations with the parent company that had been their home since year zero. This meant that they were now free to pursue other relationships, although, fittingly enough, it wasn't long before they were back at Sony again.

Stop the Clocks was preceded by an EP on 13th November, which consisted of the tracks: Acquiesce, Cigarettes & Alcohol (demo), Some Might Say (live 1995), and The Masterplan. Because it had four tracks, the EP was not eligible for the UK Official Singles Chart, perhaps hinting at how bands and record companies were starting to look at ways of diversifying content to cope with the pressures of the internet. The album proper was released a week later, just in time for the Christmas market.

Best-of Album 1:

Stop the Clocks
Released: 20th November 2006; UK Chart Position: 2;
Label: Big Brother
Track Listing:
Disc one: Rock 'n' Roll Star; Some Might Say (edited version); Talk Tonight; Lyla; The Importance of Being Idle; Wonderwall; Slide Away (alternate mix); Cigarettes & Alcohol; The Masterplan
Disc two: Live Forever; Acquiesce; Supersonic; Half the World Away; Go Let It Out; Songbird (L Gallagher); Morning Glory; Champagne Supernova; Don't Look Back in Anger
Producers: Dave Batchelor, Mark Coyle, Owen Morris, Mike Stent, Dave Sardy, Oasis

---

"Did someone say Westlife? That goes to prove there is no God!" said Noel Gallagher mid-set in the Union Chapel on 26th November 2006, having just found out that the Irish boyband had beaten Oasis to the top spot of the charts. At number 2, Oasis were one spot higher than their beloved Beatles though, which must have been something of a comfort. The Beatles *Love* album was a reimagining of some of their best-loved tracks by producer George Martin and his son Giles for the Cirque du Soleil Beatles' show.

Top of the singles chart the week that *Stop the Clocks* went to number 2 were Take That and Patience. In 1995, Take That had been one of Oasis' key chart rivals, their mainstream pop sensibilities just as keenly tuned as Oasis' indie-rock credentials, making for an interesting match in the charts. And here they were facing off again. But where Patience was Take That's first single after ten years of exile, Oasis had never gone away. Ultimately, Take That have stacked up 12 number 1 singles and eight number 1 albums; versus Oasis' eight number 1 singles and eight number 1 albums.

UK Official Albums Chart – Top 10 – 26th November 2006:

1. *The Love Album* – Westlife
2. ***Stop the Clocks* – Oasis**
3. *Love* – The Beatles
4. *U218 Singles* – U2
5. *Twenty-Five* – George Michael
6. *High Time: Singles 1992-2006* – Jamiroquai
7. *The Sound of: The Greatest Hits* – Girls Aloud
8. *Overloaded: The Singles Collection* – Sugababes
9. *Razorlight* – Razorlight
10. *Angelis* – Angelis

Although best-ofs had always been popular at this time of year, the decline in CD sales as the new millennium marched on meant that more were pumped into the market place by the record companies in an effort to shift more units. Although the inclusion of downloads and streaming in the charts was just around the corner, to see eight best-of albums in the top 10 at the end of November 2006 paints something of a bleak picture for new UK music.

The Chart Paradox

Oasis' commander-in-chief ended up presiding over the track listing of *Stop the Clocks* – the best-of that Noel swore would never happen – figuring that if it was going to be done anyway, it should at least be him in control.

There was a certain repetitive karma that it charted in second place to a boyband whose raison d'être was to rerecord Total Eclipse of the Heart for a new generation of teenage girls whose mothers had bought it the first time around. It was like coming second to Blur in 1995, and then turning around and taking over the world. Or Robbie Williams' Angels peaking at just number 4, but then going on to become one of the most successful single releases for the proceeding twenty-five years.

Perhaps most famously, Mariah Carey's 1994 single All I Want for Christmas Is You reached number 2 in both the UK and USA. Since then it has become the biggest selling Christmas single by a female artist, earning some US$16m in royalties, and has been in the UK charts for 99 weeks. In 2019 it finally reached number 1 in the Billboard Top 100, in the UK, it again reached number 2 that same year, having also done so in 2018 and 2017.

The gap between numbers 1 and 2 is enormous, a gulf wider than that between 2 and 3, or even 2 and 100, and the kudos associated with a single reaching number 1 is completely out of proportion with its subsequent chart success. This creates a strange paradox that sits at the heart of what makes the charts so fascinating. Chart success can only build a song's success so much. Songs that have charted relatively low have gone on to gain legendary status when the artist plays them live, by their inclusion in a TV show or film, or just through simple longevity in lower reaches of the charts.

Travis' 1999 single Why Does it Always Rain on Me?, for example, provided a marked upturn in the band's career, but it only charted at number 10 and spent just eight weeks on the chart. The album it was taken from, *The Man Who*, reached number 1 the week after the single first charted, spending the next two years on the chart. It had been released three months earlier and many had thought its chart life was already over.

A Lifetime's Achievement

In February 2007, Oasis were presented with the Outstanding Contribution to Music award at the Brits, honouring their 13 years as recording artists and their impact on the UK music scene. Comedian Russell Brand presented the award, joking that as a band they "stood on the shoulders of giants ... mainly because they were copying chord structures", but then adding that they were "a good band, with good haircuts" and were "natural born rock stars, true to their roots throughout their career [and] they have written anthems for a generation".

The Oasis line-up – Liam, Noel, Gem, Andy Bell and Zak Starkey (who played live but didn't join the others in collecting the award) – made their way onto the stage to the sounds of Fuckin' in the Bushes and Liam announcing, "Seeing as we don't get nominated for this shit anymore, this'll have to do". Noel added: "Thank you to anyone that has bought any of our records or come to see us live. All that's left to say is, it's been a fucking pleasure."

The band then played a twenty-minute set that included Cigarettes and Alcohol, The Meaning of Soul, and Morning Glory. When the TV programme finished airing, they continued with Don't Look Back in Anger, and Rock 'n' Roll Star.

It was as if the last twelve years hadn't happened and it was still 1995. The band were in the same explosive mood as when Liam sang "shite-life" and Noel thanked Tony Blair. It also provided a marked point of reflection for the band: were things finally beginning to draw to a close? It was not the end of the band, but it was the beginning of the end.

The band began recording their seventh studio album *Dig Out Your Soul* at Abbey Road studios in August 2007. Finally, Noel would get to record a whole album within the same hallowed halls as The Beatles, having had to abandon the *Be Here Now* sessions in 1997 because of the overwhelming press attention. This would be the last album with Zak on drums – he left the band as soon as it was finished, replaced for live duties by Chris Sharrock formerly of The La's – and also the last time the band would ever record together as Oasis 2.0. Dave Sardy was once again producing and the creative elements were divided up in a similar fashion to *Don't Believe the Truth*, with each of the four members contributing songs, although Noel led the charge, penning six of the 11 tracks.

Recording was a relatively easy and enjoyable experience for everyone, and with a pioneering new record deal – the band had resigned with Sony BMG (with Warners taking the North American rights), giving them more control over their release schedule and a higher royalty – it was certainly not in anyone's mind that this would be the last time they would record together. They were in the studio for four months, finishing in time for Christmas 2007.

Single 23:

Lord Don't Slow Me Down
Released: 21st October 2007; UK Chart Position: 10
(download only); Label: Big Brother; Album: *n/a*
B-sides: Meaning of Soul (live) [L Gallagher/Archer];
Don't Look Back in Anger (live)
Producers: Dave Sardy, Noel Gallagher

While they were recording the new album, Lord Don't Slow Me Down was released as a stand-alone single.

It was their first non-album single since Whatever in December 1994, and was unique for an Oasis release as it was download only. It managed to reach number 10 in the singles chart, the band's lowest placing since Live Forever in August 1994.

UK Official Singles Chart – Top 10 – 28th October 2007:

1. Bleeding Love – Leona Lewis
2. Rule the World – Take That
3. The Heart Never Lies – McFly
4. About You Now – Sugababes
5. Valerie – Mark Ronson ft. Amy Winehouse
6. Gimme More – Britney Spears
7. Apologize – Timbaland ft. One Republic
8. Uninvited – Freemasons ft. Bailey Tzuke
9. Goodbye Mr A – Hoosiers
10. **Lord Don't Slow Me Down – Oasis**

With physical sales decreasing since the late nineties, the UK began a download only chart in 2004, which was eventually incorporated into the main chart in 2005. Even though downloads represented the vast majority of the singles that qualified for the charts by October 2007, it was still something of an achievement for Oasis to reach number 10 on download only.

Plus, in a similar fashion to the Stop the Clocks EP, the single was released to promote the release of the tour documentary of the same name, released on DVD on 29th October 2007.

Lord Don't Slow Me Down, film (Walsh, 2007)

Shot in stilted, grainy black and white, Baillie Walsh's film follows the band from March to May 2005 as they traverse the globe on their *Don't Believe the Truth* world tour. Similar in style and tone to Grant Gee's ground-breaking claustrophobic 1998 Radiohead tour documentary, *Meeting People is Easy*, the warts-and-all doc shows the band waiting nervously backstage as anticipation builds for their Madison Square Garden show in New York. Liam rubs KY Jelly on his in-ear monitors, Noel pretends to hide his face from the kitchen staff they pass en route to the stage (á la *Spinal Tap*), and then comes the burst of adrenaline as Rock 'n' Roll Star launches into life.

Jumping from gig to party to interview, just like the tour itself, the film documents Noel being mistaken for Liam on Italian radio (in Italian), captures the heavily jet-lagged Gallagher brothers bickering in a Japanese hotel bar, Liam abandoning a photo shoot to introduce himself to a spying Girls Aloud, Noel dodging a heavily inebriated Charlotte Church backstage at the Millennium Stadium in Cardiff, and Tom Meighan from support band Kasabian dancing around the band's dressing room sharing his feelings for Tom Cruise and footballer Michael Owen.

With no talking heads, no captions noting who everyone is, and no voiceover, Walsh's light-touch style is unobtrusive, giving new meaning to fly-on-the-wall, and finding influence in the work of the great American documentary maker Fred Wiseman (famed for letting his subject matter speak for itself). The schoolboy antics and macho-competitiveness of the film's subjects reveal a group of lads who could be anywhere: drinking, laughing, arguing, and always watching football as their huge tour-machine moves seamlessly from city to city. The size of the gigs and the band's level of fame is only obvious from the crowds that gather at the concerts and below the hotel windows, and from the fleets of 4x4s used to whisk them all away afterwards like visiting dignitaries.

Like the famous journalist-scrum scene from the Beatles' film *A Hard Day's Night*, it seems the only place the guys can get any semblance of peace is backstage. Whenever they are in public, they are being hounded by fans, reporters or sycophants, all desperate to ask the exact same question: what is the state of the relationship between Noel and Liam? Each band member behaves with the utmost professionalism (even Liam); whether they are sitting through endless radio or TV interviews, or posing for pictures with fans, they are always happy to oblige.

The film constantly reminds us though that this is a working band. In one scene Gem Archer and Andy Bell work with acoustic guitars, while the rest of the group watch a football match in the room next door. Later, they all compete in an unseen improvised board game, the complicated rules presumably invented to work under any conditions, helping to stave off the hours of monotony while travelling. Predictably, Noel wins.

This is a different Oasis to the legendary party boys of the early days, and even when Noel promises to get "seriously fucked" at an after-show party, he ends up sitting quietly drinking a glass of red wine while Liam's girlfriend Nicole, her friends and the band's crew, chat amicably in the hallway.

Rather, it is the music that the maturing band are deliberately focused on. Noel comments that they are making sure they enjoy their current success because, unlike the late nineties, they'll actually be able to remember it. But their customary dry wit and irreverent humour are still a key part of the band's existence. The opening sequence sees half the band and their road crew struggling to open a huge bottle of champagne, before

Noel steps to the foreground, shakes his head and opts to open a much smaller one.

Before the documentary is over there are more gigs, more interviews and more awards ceremonies, the latter underlining the renewed success brought by *Don't Believe the Truth*, which wins best album at the 2005 Q Awards. In the film's most poignant moment, Noel sits alone, high up in the stand behind the stage as the Millennium Stadium slowly fills with fans. The scene is purposefully juxtaposed with a post-concert party featuring Charlotte Church, where Noel attempts to placate the fame-hungry hordes, desperate for a piece of him. Walsh artfully shows that, despite being a rock star, Noel is still careful to make sure he is in touch with the people who put him there in the first place. It is not just rhetoric when Noel thanks the people who voted for the Q Award for album of the year, he really means it. If nothing else, this documentary shows a group fully aware of who put them where they are, and who could take it away again.

Single 24:

The Shock of the Lightning
Released: 29th September 2008; UK Chart Position: 3;
Label: Big Brother; Album: *Dig Out Your Soul*
B-sides: Falling Down (Chemical Brothers remix)
Producers: Dave Sardy, Noel Gallagher

The Shock of the Lightning was the first Oasis single released from a new album that didn't reach number 1 since Supersonic in 1994. It might lack the listenability of Lyla and The Hindu Times, but it is as infectious and immediate a slice of guitar indie-pop as the band ever produced. It even has a short but spirited drum solo from Zak Starkey.

UK Official Singles Chart – Top 10 – 5th October 2008:

1. So What – Pink
2. Sex on Fire – Kings of Leon
3. **The Shock of the Lightning – Oasis**
4. Girls – Sugababes
5. I Love You Anyway – Boyzone
6. Disturbia – Rihanna
7. I Kissed a Girl – Katy Perry
8. When I Grow Up – Pussycat Dolls
9. In This City – Iglu & Hartly
10. Cookie Jar – Gym Class Heroes ft. The Dream

The Shock of the Lightning went in at number 3 behind the mega-hit Sex on Fire from Kings of Leon, a band that Noel had championed since 2003. In fact, there was something of the pupil beating the master with Sex on Fire charting above Shock of the Lightning, seeing as it been released a week earlier and had reached number 1. While Shock of the Lightning was generally accepted as a further step in the band's return to form, when you're used to reaching number 1, any other chart placing feels like a failure.

This top 10 shows how chart music slowly shifts from one group of acts to another over time. Acts like Oasis and Boyzone had been releasing records since the nineties, and the Sugababes since the early noughties. Now they were slowly being replaced by Rihanna and Katy Perry and the Kings of Leon.

Album 7:

Dig Out Your Soul
Released: 6th October 2008; UK Chart Position: 1;
Label: Big Brother
Track Listing: Bag it Up; The Turning; Waiting for the Rapture; The Shock of the Lightning; I'm Outta Time

---

(L Gallagher); (Get Off Your) High Horse Lady;
Falling Down; To Be Where There's Life (Archer);
Ain't Got Nothin' (L Gallagher); The Nature of Reality
(Bell); Soldier On (L Gallagher)
Producers: Dave Sardy, Noel Gallagher

UK Official Albums Chart – Top 10 – 12th October
2008:

1. **_Dig Out Your Soul_– Oasis**
2. _Only by the Night_ – Kings of Leon
3. _Let it Go_ – Will Young
4. _Good Girl Gone Bad_ – Rihanna
5. _Songs for You Truths for Me_ – James Morrison
6. _Year of the Gentleman_ – Ne-Yo
7. _The Best Bette_ – Bette Midler
8. _One Voice_ – Andrew Johnston
9. _Tell Tale Signs: Bootleg Series vol. 8_ – Bob Dylan
10. _Rockferry_ – Duffy

Dig Out Your Soul is a solid album of indie-rock
songs, written and recorded by a rock 'n' roll band
playing at the top of their game. The song writing,
although not as democratically shared around as their
previous two albums, is still influenced by a range of
pens, with Liam's inclusions showing a marked
development (the wistful Lennon-inspired I'm Outta
Time is perhaps his finest composition).

The lyrics, guitar licks, electronic bleeps and
rising and falling melodies are all present and correct, but
there is the nagging feeling that we have been here
before. Sadly, this is no _Abbey Road_. It is not the classic
final record that a band somehow produces after
everyone thinks they are done. Instead, it is the last
hurrah of a band on the verge of splitting up (more like
Let it Be). Where _Don't Believe the Truth_ felt innovative and

160

fresh, *Dig Out Your Soul*, as the name suggests, finds the band mining old ideas, completely ignoring the fact that repeating the same task and expecting a different result is the definition of insanity.

With six song-writing credits, Noel once again positions himself as the band's driving force, displaying a continued commitment to creating new music, but the first three tracks on the album – Bag It Up, The Turning and Waiting for the Rapture – though listenable enough, sound like he is phoning-in what the listener might expect an Oasis song to sound like. It is as if he is in a hurry to get through the tracks and on to the stuff he finds more interesting, like Falling Down or (Get Off Your) High Horse Lady; tracks he would rather sing himself than give to his brother. The Turning even includes a line that was surely meant for Waiting for the Rapture ("then come on, when the rapture takes me"), confusing the listener even further.

With Noel's dominance of the album, Liam's contributions, and to a lesser extent those of Archer and Bell, suggest that the record is pulling in two distinct directions.

Looking at the track titles, the band appear, perhaps subconsciously, to be aware that they are heading towards the end, even if the subject has not yet been voiced. I'm Outta Time, Falling Down, and Bag it Up all refer to literal endings, while Waiting for the Rapture, Ain't Got Nothin, and The Nature of Reality take a more philosophical tack, and the somewhat dishearteningly named Soldier On discusses the looming end and new beginning facing two old comrades:

> *Who's to say,*
> *That you were right,*
> *And I was wrong,*
> *Soldier on.*

Come the day,
Come the night,
I'll be gone,
Soldier on.

The song sees Liam in an uncharacteristically philosophical mood, penning a final sombre epitaph to the band. It suggests that the individual fights between the two brothers never mattered but, cumulatively, they signalled the end of whatever special thing it was that the brothers bought to the band. Rather than trying to soldier on, the song suggests it's time to move on.

Single 25:

I'm Outta Time (L Gallagher)
Released: 1ˢᵗ December 2008; UK Chart Position: 12;
Label: Big Brother; Album: *Dig Out Your Soul*
B-sides: I'm Outta Time (Twiggy Ramirez remix)
[L Gallagher]; The Shock of the Lightning (Jagz Kooner remix)
Producers: Dave Sardy, Noel Gallagher

Liam's developing song writing abilities are ably shown on *Dig Out Your Soul*, which contains one of his finest compositions. I'm Outta Time is one of the high points on the album, and an obvious choice for the second single, as it wraps itself in nostalgia, "looking back at the things that we have done", in a similar way to The Beatles' Free as a Bird did 1995. Its title is a clear indicator that Liam was only too aware that the band's days were numbered, with lines like "it's getting hard to fly" signposting his feelings about the changes to come. The song is an understated gem – even Noel called it "deceptively brilliant".

I'm Outta Time reached number 12 in the UK Official Singles Chart at the beginning of December 2008, the band's lowest chart placing since Supersonic. Did this mean that the song was a worse composition than, say, Sunday Morning Call, which reached number 4? Certainly not. It did signify that the band's success was waning though, and that people were looking for other acts to buy, download and stream, which slowly pushed the band toward their decision to split less than a year later. They failed to include any B-sides on the single, making it feel like they were marking time: bands release singles, so we better put one out. Instead, the single included two alternate mixes: a stark, stripped back version of the lead track from producer Dave Sardy and former Marilyn Manson guitarist Twiggy Ramirez, and a new take on The Shock of the Lightning by Jagz Kooner.

UK Official Singles Chart – Top 10 – 7th December 2008:

1. Run – Leona Lewis
2. Greatest Day – Take That
3. Womanizer – Britney Spears
4. Hot n Cold – Katy Perry
5. Human – The Killers
6. If I Were a Boy – Beyonce
7. Live Your Life – Ti ft. Rihanna
8. Right Now (Na Na Na) – Akon
9. The Boy Does Nothing – Alesha Dixon
10. Use Somebody – Kings of Leon

....

12. I'm Outta Time – Oasis

Leona Lewis was number 1 on 1st December 2008 with her cover of Snow Patrol's 2004 hit single, Run. She had won the third series of X-Factor in 2006 and was the best and most successful act to come out of the show to date. Having attended the Brit School alongside the likes of Adele and Amy Whitehouse, she stood head and shoulders above her fellow contestants on the show, and, win or lose, her success was all but secured anyway.

This was not the greatest week for rock 'n' roll. But it is probably important to note that streaming and downloading meant new work from an act often pushes their older songs back up the charts again. Lewis, Beyonce, Katy Perry, Take That, and Akon all had up to three songs in the top 100. Similarly, cover versions push the originals back up the charts as well. Lewis' cover of Run, for example, not only pushed the Snow Patrol original back into the top 30, four years after its original release, but also helped propel their other huge single Chasing Cars back into the chart that same week. A similar pattern emerges every Christmas now too, as favourite old festive songs flood the charts without band's actually having to rerelease them for the umpteenth time.

Some argue that this skews the charts, misrepresenting a list of what should predominantly be new music. But it does provide an accurate representation of what fans are actually listening to, thus diminishing the power of the record companies.

With a simple yet classic Noel guitar riff that locks in with the driving tom-tom heavy drum line, Falling Down's four chord progression – based once again around Noel's much-loved Em7 – suggests a move away from anthemic choruses toward the more subtle melody lines he would favour on his first solo album.

Single 26:

Falling Down
Released: 9th March 2009; UK Chart Position: 10;
Label: Big Brother; Album: *Dig Out Your Soul*

B-sides: Those Swollen Hand Blues; Falling Down
(demo)
Producers: Dave Sardy, Noel Gallagher

Just like his early solo singles, Everybody's on the Run and AKA… What a Life!, Falling Down, sang of course by Noel, shares a subtle yet urgent drive, completely at odds with the stadium filling chants of Acquiesce and Don't Look Back in Anger.

This makes it an interesting choice as the band's final single (although they were presumably not fully aware it was their final single at the time), but the perfect choice all the same. With his song writing clearly still developing, it is obvious, even in 2009, that Noel was already looking forward to what he, rather than Oasis, might produce next.

UK Official Singles Chart – Top 10 – 15th March 2009:

1. Islands in the Stream – Jenkins/West/Jones/Gibb
2. Right Round – Flo Rida ft. Kesha
3. Just Can't Get Enough – The Saturdays
4. Poker Face – Lady Gaga
5. Love Story – Taylor Swift
6. My Life Would Suck Without You – Kelly Clarkson
7. Dead and Gone – Ti ft. Justin Timberlake
8. Use Somebody – Kings of Leon
9. Beautiful – Akon ft. K. Offishall/C. O'Donis
10. **Falling Down – Oasis**

The week that Falling Down went straight in at number 10, the number 1 single was by Tom Jones, Ruth Jones and Rob Brydon, the latter two as Nessa and Uncle Bryn from the sitcom *Gavin and Stacey*, singing Dolly

Parton's Islands in the Stream to raise money for Comic Relief.

As this was Oasis' last single, the second wave of Britpop was now fully over and, by their final death knell in August 2009, guitar music relinquished its hold on the charts. There were, however, a handful of resilient indie-rock acts who continued releasing hit albums in 2009, including White Lies, Franz Ferdinand, Fleet Foxes, and The View. Plus, new work from old stalwarts like Morrissey and Bruce Springsteen.

Only Kings of Leon experienced anything close to the success of Oasis though, with their third album *Only by the Night* dropping in an out of the top spot on its initial mega run of 148 weeks on the chart.

With the one-two hit of Liam's I'm Outta Time and Noel's Falling Down, the last two singles released by Oasis brought a fitting end to the band's recorded releases. I'm Outta Time suggested that the younger brother, living in his older sibling's song writing shadow for so long, was now ready to forge his own way; while Noel's composition suggested a move away from the group he had made his name with.

CHAPTER ELEVEN
This is the End, and This is the Beginning (2009-2020)

In March 2007, fresh from the band's Outstanding Contribution to Music Brit Award, Noel performed his biggest solo show to date to eight thousand people at the Royal Albert Hall. Although he had been performing chunks of Oasis' live set solo since the band's earliest days, his relaxed confidence taking centre stage at such a major venue was a strong indication that he might be interested in a world outside of Oasis, and perhaps more importantly, that the world might be interested in him as a solo act. It is often assumed that the songwriter of a group will go on to have a successful solo career but, as in the case of Gary Barlow and Take That, it is not always guaranteed.

The Dreams of Children concert, in aid of the Teenage Cancer Trust, was named after a song by The Jam, and was one of Noel's more subtle lyrical lifts, appearing in the B-side Fade Away: "The dreams we have as children, fade away." The epic acoustic set included Oasis classics, such as Fade Away and Listen Up, as well as Wonderwall and Half the World Away, and covers of The Smiths' There is a Light That Never Goes Out, The Beatles' All You Need is Love, and a guest appearance "all the way from the bar" from Paul Weller on his own track, The Butterfly Collector.

Back in the world of Oasis, the band continued to tour *Dig Out Your Soul* in 2009, playing the UK, the USA, Europe, Japan, South Africa, China, South-East Asia and South America. The inertia that a long tour instils in a group, combined with the comfort a behemoth act like Oasis experience on the road, kept them trucking on, meaning their old issues did not surface until they were back in the UK in the summer of 2009. The combined weight of the arguments could be ignored no longer.

The final split came backstage on 28th August 2009, ninety minutes before the band were due on at the Festival Rock en Seine, on the outskirts of Paris. A week earlier the band had been forced to cancel a gig at the V Festival at short notice because Liam contracted laryngitis. Noel had publicly called him out on the decision, knowing full well how he had flaked out of concerts in the past, and Liam had threatened to sue him (providing a sick note from his doctor). Noel had retracted his accusation, but their mutual animosity raised its head again backstage in Paris. Noel had finally had enough of his brother's inflammatory antics and left the group then and there, leaving Madness to headline the festival in their place. Two hours later, Noel published the following statement on the band's website:

> *It is with some sadness and great relief ... I quit Oasis tonight. People will write and say what they like, but I simply could not go on working with Liam a day longer.*

And the brothers haven't really spoken since. With Noel gone there was no question of Oasis continuing, such was the weight of his presence, and the band's final gig was on 20th August 2009 at the rather unglamorous Bridlington Spa, ending not with a bang but with a whimper. There was one final encore, however, in the form of another best-of album, reminding fans just how great their music had been. This also meant that Sony would finally get to put out the best-of that they wanted to.

Having released *Stop the Clocks* just three years earlier, *Time Flies… 1994-2009* covers much of the same material. It is comprised of the band's 26 singles (27 tracks with the double A-side of She is Love/Little by Little), without any album tracks or B-sides. For most bands, a greatest hits and a singles collection are much the same thing, but *Stop the Clocks* includes the likes of Talk Tonight, Half the World Away and The Masterplan, while *Time Flies...* has Who Feels Love? and Go Let it Out. Both albums had their pluses and minuses, but at least Oasis managed to avoid being accused of flogging a dead horse by releasing numerous best-ofs, all with variations of the same songs. Stand up please U2.

Best of Album 2:

Time Flies... 1994-2009
Released: 14th June 2010; UK Chart Position: 1; Label: Big Brother
Track Listing:
Disc 1: Supersonic; Roll With It; Live Forever; Wonderwall; Stop Crying Your Heart Out; Cigarettes & Alcohol; Songbird (L Gallagher); Don't Look Back in Anger; The Hindu Times; Stand By Me; Lord Don't Slow Me Down; Shakermaker; All Around the World
Disc 2: Some Might Say; The Importance of Being Idle; D'You Know What I Mean; Lyla; Let There Be Love; Go Let It Out; Who Feels Love?; Little By Little; The Shock of the Lightning; She is Love; Whatever; I'm Outta Time (L Gallagher); Falling Down; Sunday Morning Call
Producers: Dave Batchelor, Mark Coyle, Owen Morris, Mike Stent, Dave Sardy, Oasis

---

UK Official Albums Chart – Top 10 – 20ᵗʰ June 2009:

1. ***Time Flies… 1994-2009* – Oasis**
2. *Glee, The Music: Journey to Regionals* – The Cast of Glee
3. *Crazy Love* – Michael Bublé
4. *The Very Best of* – Glenn Miller
5. *In the Mood* – RAF Squadronaires
6. *The Element of Freedom* – Alicia Keys
7. *Piano Man: The Very Best of* – Billy Joel
8. *The Fame* – Lady Gaga
9. *The Defamation of Strickland Banks* – Plan B
10. *Sigh No More* – Mumford & Sons

Released into a mixed bag of a mid-year album chart, *Time Flies…* succeeded where *Stop the Clocks* failed by reaching the top spot. The cast of the TV show *Glee* were at number 2 with an album that included three Journey covers (Faithfully, Anyway You Want it, and the shows key signifier Don't Stop Believing), plus Queen's Bohemian Rhapsody, Lulu's To Sir With Love, and the old standard Over the Rainbow.

Despite being a full six months until Christmas, there were a further 25 best-of albums in the top 100, including a remarkable four more Glee collections, all consisting of just four or five tracks, designed to represent a different point in the fictional show choir's career.

It seemed Oasis were bowing out at precisely the time they were needed the most. Even now, the likes of Supersonic, Roll With It, Some Might Say, Live Forever, and even the newer material such as Stop Crying Your Heart Out make the album sound current and so urgent, as if they were written just yesterday. Liam's voice has never sounded so gritty and full of life, and Noel's songs are as incendiary as ever. The best-of does what best-ofs were designed to do: remind fans, and those discovering the music for the first time, just what fantastic songs the band had.

We're Outta Time

Sometime after the band split, Noel expressed regret that the end came the way it did and wondered aloud – like a spurned lover who misses the intimacy of a relationship – whether they could somehow have found a way to stay together. Fans grasped at this statement, which suggested, to no one more than Liam himself, that the decision to split might not be as final as he had once made it out to be. So far, fans are still hoping, probably in vain. Noel seems content to work solo, and Liam – although continually suggesting on social media that the band should get back together – is also experiencing reinvigorated success on his own terms.

The closer you look at their last album, the more it appears as an epitaph to their career, suggesting that Noel was really addressing his regret at the way the band fell apart. Liam's volatile behaviour aside, Noel managed to keep a pretty strong rein on Oasis' over the years, but the fact that they had to cancel a handful of gigs after splitting so suddenly meant there were disappointed fans unable to see the band play.

Noel always understood that Oasis' success was only ever made possible because of the fans, and he felt guilty that many missed the chance to see them play live. Liam understood this too, but was loathe to express it. While Noel thanked everyone who had bought their records or seen them live in his acceptance speech for the Outstanding Contribution to Music Brit Award in 2007, Liam focused on the fact that they were no longer nominated for Brit Awards, exposing his fear that the band were no longer relevant. For all his public posturing about his own excellence, Noel always understood who it was that made him successful – it was always his greatest strength. Although the music would always be available to listen to, he knew he was going to miss the band connecting with the audience on an emotional level: playing live.

Perhaps more than anything, Oasis songs are about the joint experience, the anthemic choruses designed for fans to sing along to just as if they were on the football terraces, or to lose themselves to as they once did in the Haçienda. The band were rarely animated on stage, but this only made them more real for their fans. This was not a group who put on a show to be watched from beyond a fourth wall; they invited their audience to join them, even wearing the same casual clothes like a uniform. They learnt this from their forebears The Stone Roses and the Happy Mondays, particularly the latter who often looked like they had just wandered on stage from the audience – creating a new band hybrid and blurring the lines between audience and group.

It was impossible for The Beatles to connect properly with their audience live because most of their fans were under the age of sixteen and no one could hear the band play over their screams. That is not to say they were not a band for the people though, with anthems like All You Need is Love delivering a simple message of unity. It is no coincidence that Noel and Paul Weller played the song at the *Dreams of Children* concert, as Noel strongly identified with the Beatles' music and used it as the starting point in creating Oasis. When it came to playing live, Oasis were able to experience more success than their heroes because of the technological advancements that made huge concerts possible, and the development in what fans expected from their shows.

As a band, Radiohead were the antithesis of Oasis. The experimental guitar band, who began to experience their biggest period of success with the release of their third album *OK Computer* in May 1997, just as Oasis' star was on the wane, were all about the individual. In a similar way to other champions of the dispossessed such as Morrissey, Radiohead's music reached out to those who lacked the confidence to speak up for themselves. This meant their concerts attracted singular loners, which, ironically, gave them a collective identity.

Even as their fortunes began to slide, Oasis' concerts maintained their massive scale. They always headlined festivals and played stadiums rather than halls, even in America where they sold out Madison Square Garden in New York in 2005. The warmth and unity of their concert-going fans meant they maintained their loyal fanbase throughout, like a football team, even after a line-up change. Come August 2009, this must have been hard for the band to give up.

So, What Next?

In some respects, Oasis did continue to play together after they split up. They just went under the name Beady Eye and were without their leader and chief songwriter (or any of their songs). By November 2009, the other three (with Chris Sharrock on drums) had announced there would be new material in 2010. In fact, the first of the band's two albums – the aptly named *Different Gear, Still Speeding* – didn't see the light of day until February 2011. Which in music terms, was still incredibly quick.

The project's speedy turnaround was a result of the comfortable place the band had reached playing together. Liam's confidence in his own song writing was growing, and Gem and Andy had been playing together for ten years by this point. Comfort, however, is a notoriously dangerous place in rock 'n' roll, and after Noel called them "Stratford's finest Oasis tribute band"[xxxv] when they played Wonderwall at the 2012

London Olympics closing ceremony, it was clear they were not getting his endorsement.

A million tiny things are needed to make a band truly great. There was nothing wrong with most of the songs written by Liam, Gem and Andy, but there was nothing great about them either. In the end, Beady Eye positioned themselves as a modern rock 'n' roll supergroup like Audioslave or Velvet Revolver, whose material was fine, but did not compare to their former glories.

To his credit, Liam was aware of his limitations as a song writer and by the time he recorded his first solo album, *As You Were*, in 2017, he had hired hit-making producers Greg Kurstin, Andrew Wyatt and Dan Grech-Marguerat to help him realise his vision.

Many considered this a canny move, but not Noel. Despite taking the high ground and remaining largely silent on his brother's antics post-Oasis, he just couldn't help himself, refusing to acknowledge Liam's solo efforts because he didn't write the songs himself. Did Elvis write his own material, Noel? Even some of the greatest song writers shared writing credits, such as David Bowie, who wrote with producer Brian Eno.

Liam's decision to accept help proved advantageous though; the result was two albums of solid rock songs that saw a resurgence in the fate of Gallagher junior. Both debuted at number 1 in the UK Official Albums Chart, *As You Were* being joined by *Why Me Why Not* in 2019. More recently, Liam has returned to playing live again, his own compositions sitting comfortably alongside his favourite Oasis songs such as Cast No Shadow, Rock 'n' Roll Star and Morning Glory.

Twenty-three years after crying off at the last minute, Liam finally got to play *MTV Unplugged* in August 2019. He was even joined on stage by Bonehead, who, Liam pointed out, is one of the few people in history to have played *MTV Unplugged* twice. His set was packed with his solo material and Oasis classics, including Sad Song (a track that Noel originally sang) which he dedicated to Oasis. The album of the concert was released on 12th June 2020 and went straight in at the top spot, giving Liam three number 1s in a row.

Noel slipped seamlessly into his solo career as if he had been preparing for it for years. Which he had. Like all great song writers, he understood that he needed to develop and evolve if he was going to remain at the top of his game, so, after 2011's *Noel Gallagher's High Flying Birds* and 2015's *Chasing Yesterday*, 2017's *Who Built the Moon?* took a sharp turn toward the experimental with Noel drafting in electro-pioneer producer David Holmes to help create something new.

Rather than simply adding drum loops and keyboard bleeps, the songs on *Who Built the Moon?* take their time, using the structures of elongated dance remixes alongside rock guitars and drums, with repeated snippets of melody lines looped like guitar riffs. Interestingly, this pushed Noel's work more towards the experimental post-*OK Computer* work of Radiohead, once the polar opposite of Oasis.

The album split his fanbase but was generally accepted as a big step forward in development for him as a musician. Those put off by the sample loops were still given the retro Northern Soul stylings of the first single, the tub-thumping Holy Mountain. And Noel always remembered his roots; at the heart of all the techno loops and layered samples there often sits a song that would sound equally good played on an acoustic guitar. Nowhere is this more true than on the bonus track to *Who Built the Moon?*, recorded live during a sound-check and mostly made up on the spot. Dead in the Water is a classic heartfelt ballad dripping with pure primal emotion, reminiscent of early Oasis acoustic ballads like Take Me

Away, linking Noel's solo career with the very first single he released.

Who Built the Moon? was followed by a run of similarly styled singles throughout 2019 and 2020, including Black Star Dancing, This is the Place and Blue Moon Rising. The track Come on Outside includes the line, "The voices in your head get so loud, 'cause your problems are the size of a cow", showing that Noel's penchant for lifting lyrics from other songs has not yet disappeared despite him being in his fifties.

Don't Stop… Demo

And then something happened that many thought would never. But not quite in the way that fans expected. On 24th April 2020, a new Oasis song was released. Don't Stop… was sung by Noel and was recorded around 2006/7, originally intended to be on one of the band's last two albums. Appearing in demo format, and with just a strummed acoustic, simple picked electric guitars and light percussion, the song is similar to Half the World Away and Talk Tonight.

It is not clear why it was originally kept from release or why it was only put out in 2020, but on the strength of streaming alone it reached number 80 in the UK Official Singles Chart.

UK Official Singles Chart – Top 10 – 8th May 2020:

1. Tootsie Slide – Drake
2. Say So – Doja Cat
3. Savage – Megan Thee Stallion
4. Death Bed – Powfu ft. Beabadoobee
5. Blinding Lights – The Weeknd
6. Rockstar – Dababy ft. Roddy Ricch
7. Rover – Simba ft. DTG

Liam and Noel – the Heart of the Star

In 2018, the satirical animated sitcom *Family Guy* included
a sketch where "two toothless British homeless people
have filthy sex in an alleyway and become the
grandparents of the guys from Oasis." The scene is then
accompanied by an image of a near identical Liam and
Noel circa 1997 in which they don't even look their most
dishevelled. This sketch highlights how the world saw –
and continues to see – Oasis; not just as dirty, scruffy
and, well, tramp-like, but also, how similar they consider
the brothers to be. Oasis fans would disagree.

In *Supersonic*, Noel states that he doesn't
understand how he and Liam have turned out so different
when they shared the same upbringing. So alike do many
consider the brothers to be, that they are often confused
for one another, just like the scene in the Italian radio
show in *Lord Don't Slow Me Down* in which Noel dryly
looks around for his brother after being introduced as
him. This strange juxtaposition remains at the heart of
what made Oasis so engaging. They at once seemed to be
one of the tightest little gangs in town, while
simultaneously pulling in opposite directions, harnessing a
strange kind of schizophrenia that continually left the
world wondering what they would do next.

Take their most famous song, Wonderwall. It is a
love song that consists of a simple, gentling lilting
melody. When Noel sings the song solo he strips it right
back, just as Ryan Adams does on his haunting, reverb-
drenched cover on his 2004 album *Love is Hell* (recorded

after Adams toured with Oasis in America). But with Liam's voice, and his personality, Wonderwall takes on another personality entirely. Liam's voice is loud, confident, brash, but also accurate; he hits the right notes and holds them, giving the song its clearest identity (and its phenomenal success). Everything else is backing. For Oasis to succeed, the band needed both brothers.

Liam always brought an exciting primal energy to the band's live shows, while Noel's solo sections created a completely different vibe: a show within a show. Liam preferred to prowl the stage, limiting his banter to the odd word or semi-articulate phrase, which created a stark visual identity. He was the embodiment of the band's early tracks, Rock 'n' Roll Star and Cigarettes and Alcohol, preferring to let the music speak for itself, a hulk of brooding masculinity akin to Marlon Brandon's Stanley Kowalski in *A Streetcar Named Desire*. Noel, aware that he didn't exude the same primal masculinity as his brother, preferred to connect with his audience through stories and jokes between the songs. Bands generally go for one or the other of these on-stage personalities; Oasis took on both, the visual and the audio working in tandem.

Before Noel discovered his own on-stage style, and fully aware of the attention that Liam drew, Oasis originally relied almost exclusively on Liam's brooding character for their visual identity. When Johnny Marr saw them play for the first time in Manchester, three months or so before Alan McGee did, he noted that the attitude was there already, even though no one knew who they were. He says in his autobiography:

> He *[Liam] sauntered over to the middle of the stage with his nose in the air and was looking around at everyone quizzically while shaking a white, star-shaped tambourine for no apparent reason … 'Well,' I thought, 'if he sounds half*

as good as he thinks he looks then this is going to be interesting. [xxxvi]

Liam's keen understanding that less is more has been his trademark through his time in Oasis and his solo career. But as Noel's confidence grew over the years, his own handling of the audience became just as important. And, like a once close couple who have gone their separate ways, it is now difficult to understand how they stayed together for so long, their two styles so at odds with one another.

Liam is in love with the myth of rock 'n' roll. This is most obviously displayed in his all-encompassing obsession with John Lennon (highlighted in naming his first-born Lennon). Lennon is a rock 'n' roll martyr, a proponent of love and freedom, struck down in his prime and now heralded as a legend, his death shielding him from criticism. Would Liam idolise him so much were he still alive?

Liam is everything a rock star should be: good looking, loud mouthed, hedonistic, idolised, and effortlessly talented. He seems like an archetype while also being truly unique. There really is no one else like him, and, in many ways, he is the last of the great rock stars. There is no doubt that British music would be much duller without him. He is also a product of his time. Laddism was idolised in the nineties, much more so than in the eighties. In other words, it is unlikely that Liam could have been a star in the eighties, in the same way that Morrissey would (and did) struggle in the nineties.

Noel on the other hand is an unapologetic music fan, his latest work drawing on experimental dance music just as much as rock 'n' roll. If his solo career is anything to go by, then were it not for the drag of Liam's influence, Oasis' forays into experimentation may have come much earlier.

Noel's work with the Chemical Brothers, which dates back to the 1996 number 1 single Setting Sun, followed by 1999's Let Forever Be, started a trend of indie singers guesting on dance tracks, which blurred the lines between genres and perhaps even showed how the lines didn't matter at all. Crispian Mills from Kula Shaker sang on Narayan from the mega-hit Prodigy album *The Fat of the Land* in 1997, which also featured a guest spot from Saffron from Republica on Fuel my Fire, while Tim Burgess from the Charlatans guested twice with the Chemical Brothers, as did Bernard Sumner from New Order, appearing on Out of Control in 1999. Oasis received a lot of flack about their music being retrospective and derivative, but this was a decision made not out of ignorance, but as an active choice. They played the music that the times called for.

With Noel heading in one direction and the members of Beady Eye heading in another, it is clear that Oasis' demise was most probably on Noel's mind long before he finally called it a day. He had walked off tours before, and the band had even played without him – Gem Archer was quickly promoted to lead guitar during Champagne Supernova at the Benicassim Festival in Spain in August 2000 – but there was no Oasis without Noel, in just the same way that there was no Oasis without Liam.

The relationship between the brothers sat at the heart of the band and gave it its own distinct identity, whatever records they were releasing. There are many other bands with two brothers at the centre: The Kinks, The Black Crowes, Crowded House, AC/DC, The Beach Boys (they actually had three). But with these bands, unlike Oasis, if you take one of the brothers out of the line-up (which most of these examples have done at some point), the band still maintains its general identity.

It might have looked like the end came through a classic bust-up, but the truth is much more banal than that. The spirit of Oasis was the relationship between Liam and Noel – a relationship on the wane from day one. It was as if the end was written from the very day they began to play together. Frankly, it is incredible that they managed to stay together for as long as they did, creating music along the way – from *Definitely Maybe* and *Morning Glory* through to *Time Flies...* – that achieved so much.

The relationship between the brothers is what made Oasis such a thrilling ride, and nowhere was this more clearly expressed than in the simple, honest songs that they created together. Most bands would be happy with one classic song in the repertoire; Oasis have at least three: Wonderwall, Don't Look Back in Anger and Live Forever. Their songs were written and performed in a way that captured a moment in history, making them timeless. No one fully understands what makes a band truly great. As John Lennon said: "If we knew that, we'd all form other groups and become managers."[xxxvii] But, when it comes to British bands in the nineties, there were few as truly great as Oasis.

THE END

ABOUT THE AUTHOR

Tom Boniface-Webb is a writer and sometime filmmaker from Reading in the South-East of the United Kingdom. He currently lives in Wellington, New Zealand.

In 2017 his first non-fiction book 'I Was Britpopped: The A-Z of Britpop' was published through Valley Press, written with the co-author Jenny Natasha.

For more information about the Modern Music Masters series:
modernmusicmastersuk@gmail.com
www.modernmusicmasters.co.uk

Endnotes:

i Hook, Peter 'The Haçienda: How Not to Run a Night Club', pg. 95, itBooks (2014)

ii Nice, James 'Shadowplayers: The Rise and Fall of Factory Records' pg. 328, Aurum (2011)

iii Marr, Johnny 'Set the Boy Free' pg. 126, Century (2014)

iv Quoted in - https://www.bbc.com/news/uk-16361170

v *Joy Divison*, a film by Grant Gee (2007)

vi *Tear it Up and Start Again*, Simon Reynold, pg. 105

vii Oasis gig info - https://www.songkick.com/artists/548892-oasis/gigography?page=17

viii Nice, James 'Shadowplayers: The Rise and Fall of Factory Records', pg. 423, Aurum (2017)

ix Nice, James 'Shadowplayers: The Rise and Fall of Factory Records' Aurum (2017)

x Marr, Johnny 'Set the Boy Free', pg. 320-1, Criterion (2014)

xi Mark Arm quoted in Mojo 318, "Winner's Blues" by Keith Cameron

xii Source – https://www.telegraph.co.uk/music/artists/oasis-definitely-maybe-album-debut-facts/

xiii Harris, John 'The Last Party', pg. 175, Harper Perennial (2003)

xiv Niven, Alex 'Definitely Maybe' (33 1/3 series), pg. 22, Bloomsbury (2013)

xv Reference - https://www.theguardian.com/music/musicblog/2007/may/08/inspring2008blurandoasis

xvi Harris, John 'The Last Party', pg. 251, Harper Perennial (2003)

xvii Source: The UK Charts Database - https://www.officialcharts.com/chart-news/the-uks-biggest-studio-albums-of-all-time__24431/

xviii Cliff Jones, The Face, August 1994

xix Footage can be seen here - https://www.youtube.com/watch?v=xPBlVZNnWyk

xx Niven, Alex 'Definitely Maybe' (33 1/3 series), pg. 25, Bloomsbury (2013)

xxi Source - https://www.indiepedia.de/index.php?title=100_Greatest_British_Albums_of_All_Time_(NME,_2006)

xxii Source -
https://web.archive.org/web/20060103175527/http://www.kn
ebworthhouse.com/rock/the90s.htm
xxiii Film – *Supersonic* (Whitecross, 2016)
xxiv Rolling Stones in Hyde Park 1969 -
https://www.youtube.com/watch?v=3ku3ZQdpKQg
xxv Queen and Knebworth -
https://web.archive.org/web/20060103170525/http://www.kn
ebworthhouse.com/rock/the80s.htm
xxvi Oasis at Knebworth -
https://www.youtube.com/watch?v=JQFtmlUNU_M
xxvii In 2019, Sheeran was easily the world's most streamed artist -
https://www.statista.com/statistics/1032826/spotify-artists-
monthly-listeners-
worldwide/#:~:text=As%20of%20July%2017%2C%202019,nu
mber%20ever%20recorded%20on%20Spotify.
xxviii Source - https://www.ticketmaster.co.uk/eltonjohn
xxix Source (ironically, the Guardian) -
https://www.theguardian.com/music/2020/apr/17/gerry-
cinnamon-the-bonny-review-little-runaway-records
xxx The Britpop film – *Live Forever* (Dower, 2003)
xxxi Source - https://www.officialcharts.com/chart-news/oasis-
classic-be-here-now-claims-number-1-on-the-official-vinyl-
albums-chart__16740/
xxxii Everett, Walter, 'The Beatles as Musicians: Revolver
Through the Anthology' Oxford University Press (1999)
xxxiii James Oldham, NME, November 1998 -
https://web.archive.org/web/20000817190438/http://www.n
me.com/reviews/reviews/19980927105608reviews.html
xxxiv Liam quoted in the Oasis interviews CD, released with the
boxed set editions of their first two albums
xxxv Quoted in Guardian -
https://www.theguardian.com/music/2012/aug/15/noel-
gallagher-beady-eye
xxxvi Marr, Johnny 'Set the Boy Free' Century (2016), pg. 323
xxxvii Quoted in The Beatles Anthology, 1995

Made in the USA
Middletown, DE
14 July 2021